MEMORY BOOK

Better Memory
Every   Day
of Your Life

The Author

TANSEL ALI is one of the leading thinkers on memory in the world and two-time Australian Memory Champion. He memorised two *Sydney Yellow Pages* telephone books in only twenty-four days. That is over two thousand businesses and more than twenty-thousand digits.

He holds several memory records and has competed in the World Memory Championships in Malaysia, where he achieved the rank of Grandmaster of Memory for memorizing a randomly shuffled deck of cards in under three minutes.

Tansel has spent more than eleven years training people how to make the most of their brain in order to work more effectively. His interactive coaching style and personal experience has contributed to many success stories. A much-in-demand corporate speaker and an educator, he also conducts training sessions for organizations on Memory Training.

His iPhone and Android app, 'The 4 Most Powerful Memory Techniques' has been downloaded over one hundred thousand times around the world.

At present, he is working on a ground-breaking new project, building Asia-Australia relations by developing an Asia Literacy Framework based on the Yellow Elephant model.

Tansel Ali possesses two Masters degrees — one in information systems management and an MBA.

The YELLOW ELEPHANT

LEARN FASTER
REMEMBER MORE
REDUCE STRESS

Memory Grandmaster
Tansel Ali

Orient
Publishing
DELHI | MUMBAI | HYDERABAD

To the memory of my mother
Sabiha Ali

ISBN : 978-81-222-0570-1

The Yellow Elephant

Subject: Self-Help / Personal Growth

© Tansel Ali 2013

1st Published 2014

Published in arrangement with
Hardie Grant Publishing, Australia

Published by
Orient Publishing
(an imprint of Orient Paperbacks)
5A/8 Ansari Road, Darya Ganj, New Delhi-110 002
www.orientpublishing.com

Cover Design by Vision Studio

Printed at
Saurabh Printers Pvt. Ltd., Noida, India

Cover Printed at
Ravindra Printing Press, Delhi-110 006, India

Contents

Introduction to Memory

'The true sign of intelligence is
not knowledge but imagination.'

— ALBERT EINSTEIN

BECAUSE I'VE MEMORISED telephone books and broken memory records, most people think that I'm 'gifted' with special memory powers. This is not true. You see, I never had a brilliant memory when I was younger! In fact, I used to forget a lot in my daily life and at work. It was frustrating but I took it as normal. So when my friend Metin told me he could memorise a list of forty shopping items, I laughed and didn't believe it — until one day I tested him, and sure enough he memorised them all effortlessly. At that point, I was still sceptical. I thought he had used a trick of some sort. But there was no trick; it was not deception. He actually did memorise the list in random order. Now that he had wowed me, I had to know how to do it myself. I had no idea what I could use it for but I thought it was cool and wanted to be able to do it too. Once Metin showed me the technique, I was amazed at how easy it was to remember things.

That first small success inspired me to look for other ways to memorise things. I became interested in memorising playing cards, lists of words and numbers. Excited by my new-found skills, I discovered the Australian Memory Championships and suggested to Metin that we enter. Even if we came last, it would be a great experience, I thought, and also a chance to meet like-minded people. Upon entering the competition, we both ended up breaking several national memory records and came second and third in Australia. From that point on, I knew that I had a powerful tool to help me develop myself and also to help others. I devoted myself to helping people better themselves through the amazing ability of the mind. My knowledge of memory techniques allowed me to do that very easily. When it comes down to it, improving memory is not rocket science. Apply the techniques and be prepared to amaze yourself!

Memory and Learning

In modern society, we are asked to learn more and more new things — learning doesn't end after school or university. Yet how much of what we learn do we really retain? By not using our potential, we are travelling along unaware of the amazing things we could be achieving. Memory training and techniques such as speed reading and mind mapping can greatly increase our capacity to remember what we learn, allowing us to put it all to greater use. Although I discovered memory training after I had finished my undergraduate degree, I have since applied the strategies to my current studies and it's made me better appreciate learning.

Memory training is all about imagination. It has allowed my brain to come up with more ideas and possibilities, and hence draw out opportunities that I would not have been able to before. For instance, I became a better educator as I understand how we learn, and I developed memory concepts and techniques such as the Yellow Elephant model and the ALI method. The practice of imagination required me to learn how to create strong visuals and connections, which not only helped me to remember but also helped me to become more creative and think outside the box. Memory training formed the basis of many new skills, such as speed reading, planning, time management, communication, educating, learning and, of course, remembering! I hope that this book will assist you to develop these areas as well.

In my eleven years as a memory trainer, I haven't come across anyone — from age four through to ninety — who couldn't apply the strategies I describe in this book. Anyone with a basic imagination can use these techniques to enhance their memory. Some people tell me they have tried speed reading or improving their memory before but couldn't stick with it. There are a lot of memory and speed reading courses out there that, unfortunately, only show you the techniques without an explanation of the underlying principles. I have found that it is most important to understand how these techniques work and why. By first learning the four-step Yellow Elephant model, and then applying it along with the VAI memory principle, (visualisation, association, imagination) you will understand the theory behind the techniques and be able to work with them a lot more confidently. Of course, practice makes perfect, and in this book I give you plenty of opportunities to practise, as well as tips for how to continue to improve on your own.

Technology and Memory

Devices such as smart phones and tablets play a huge role in society today. Before these technologies were available, many people would memorise telephone numbers or to-do lists, and people had to rely on their memories more in their day-to-day activities. That being said, I don't believe technology is making our memories worse. The problem is that our collective understanding of memories has not advanced as quickly as technology — we are not taught memory techniques and advanced learning strategies. Rather than blaming technology, we should be blaming ourselves. Unfortunately, not many of the techniques in this book are taught in schools today. If they were, we would learn a lot faster — and perhaps even be more advanced.

Technology allows us to organise ourselves better and we can use it to our benefit. Combining the use of technology with memory techniques will ensure greater success in today's society. Being aware of memory techniques will help us to become more mindful and allow us to approach remembering in a whole new way.

Why Train Your Memory?

Initially, it may seem like memory techniques are only good for remembering lists, numbers and names. However, if you dig deeper into what they offer, you'll find that you can use them for just about anything in work and daily life. For example, you can use the techniques to make communication memorable and improve your engagement with staff and clients, or to improve your organisation's marketing and advertising campaigns. Once you know the strategies, you can find ways of using memory techniques for many different applications. Organisations I've worked with have solved many of their problems by looking deeper into memory and its uses.

Memory techniques can help you:
- remember telephone numbers and figures
- remember faces and names better
- learn languages better
- keep mentally fit and alert
- increase creativity

- think outside the box
- foster innovation
- create compelling presentations
- remember jokes
- read faster and remember more
- recall lines from a script
- acquire knowledge, facts and data quickly
- memorise religious texts
- increase mental agility and stamina
- improve concentration and focus
- stand out from the crowd
- increase your sense of awareness
- make effective plans
- be more productive at work
- become a better entrepreneur
- reduce stress
- increase your IQ
- study more effectively
- enhance communication skills
- become a better, more mindful leader
- get into 'the zone' through visualisation
- win competitions.

Whatever your objective is, defining and establishing your goals is the first positive step to improving your memory. Have a go at writing some goals down on a piece of paper now.

Whatever your goals are, the following techniques will have you on your way to achieving them quicker than you could imagine.

The Role of Imagination
Imagination: we all have it, we all use it, but not all of us know the power that it yields to help us do extraordinary things. If

you use your imagination, you can remember anything. It's as simple as that.

When people think of memory, they think of repetition and the stress associated with it. We can memorise things through the traditional method of repetition, or we can memorise them by using our imaginations. So really, there are two ways to remember something:

- the stressful way (repetition)
- the fun way (imagination)

I have never been excited about laborious repetition. If that's your thing, then great — repeat your life away! Otherwise, using your imagination is the best way to greatly enhance your memory and reduce the stress of repetition. Not only that, but using your imagination will actually make memorising enjoyable. If things are enjoyable, then we are engaged. And if we are engaged, we can remember more easily, and hence we end up with a better and stronger memory.

How Our Brains Function

In order to understand how memory works, we need to first take a look at how our brains function.

The right-brain/left-brain theory suggests that the right side of our brain is the imaginative or creative side, and the left side is the logical or structured side. Some people are predominantly left-brained, and others predominantly right-brained. Left-brained people are organised, good at mathematics and prefer verbal instructions, whereas right-brained people will explore their creativity more, tend to use colours more, invent stories, and are more likely to venture into the unknown. Using both sides of the brain to remember allows us to combine our logical and abstract strengths with our creative and imaginative strengths. This enables us to memorise and retain an extraordinary amount of information.

Let's say we had to remember parts of an important document. The traditional method would be to repeat the information we'd like to store in our head over and over. But where is this information stored? We know it gets stored in the brain, but there is no exact location. No specific address. In order to retain this information, we need to insert 'memory' into our brain. You can think of it like saving it to your computer memory (RAM) inside your head. The more RAM you have in your computer, the more applications it can store and the faster it can run. The same goes for your brain. However, unlike computer memory, where there is a limit to how much memory any one machine can hold, our brains have an almost infinite capacity to store information. There is almost no limit to what you can remember. You can create as many 'memory chips' in your brain as you like. We have a huge amount of space to remember everything we want to learn in this life.

Test

So, how good is your memory? Using a timer, give yourself two minutes to memorise the words below as best as you can, in order.

1. Gorilla
2. Kitchen
3. Speed
4. Flower
5. Birdcage
6. Pill
7. Savage
8. Triangle
9. Trajectory
10. Subject
11. Spain
12. Shoe
13. Fountain
14. Koala
15. Wood
16. Cartoon
17. Music
18. Litigate
19. Fire
20. Kebab

Now turn your book over, and see how many you can recall.

How many did you get correct? If you got more than seven, you are doing extremely well. Miller's Law states that the number of objects an average human being can hold in working memory is seven, plus or minus two.

Key Points

- Using your imagination is the key to improving your memory.
- Everyone has an amazing capacity to improve their memory.
- Memorising can be stressful through repetition, or fun through imagination. You choose.
- Left brain is words, numbers, structure; right brain is imagination, colour, artistic skills.
- Using both sides of the brain leads to extraordinary mental abilities.
- We can add an almost infinite number of 'memory chips' to our minds.

Principles and Techniques

Yesterday is but today's memory, and
tomorrow is today's dream.

KHALIL GIBRAN

The Yellow Elephant

'I hear and I forget. I see and
I remember. I do and I understand.'

— CONFUCIUS

DURING MY TIME AS a memory competitor, I came second four times in memory championships. It's not that I wasn't memorising enough. In fact, I was memorising more than everyone else. It was because of the number of mistakes I was making, which reduced my scores. The fact that I had done so much memorising but still wasn't winning led me to think maybe there was something wrong. It took me a while, but I finally realised that remembering something really well is not just about learning the memory techniques themselves, but also about *how* to memorise.

Developing the Yellow Elephant model allowed me to change my style of memorisation. Doing so led me to winning the next two memory championships. The difference was amazing! I didn't even have to train as much, because I could rely on remembering successfully if I applied these steps.

The Yellow Elephant Model for Processing and Decoding Information

The Yellow Elephant model explains the nature of how we process and decode information. It can be applied to anything we want to remember. The four steps below outline how this model works.

1 ABSTRACT
(I hear and I forget)

Words, numbers, complex problems, people's names, instructions, presentations and so on are often 'abstract' to us, meaning that they don't immediately make sense to us and we have to go through a process of decoding the messages so that they become information we can remember. For instance, the number list 3645828162 is not exactly meaningful. But if we break up the numbers and form a story, using a particular memory system to code it, it becomes much easier to remember. Memorising numbers is explained further in 'Memory Techniques'.

Whether you know it or not, when you understand something, you are forming images of the content in your mind and building associations with them. However, there are many times when you might have trouble decoding information or a situation. For instance, it is very common for people to forget names, because they don't form an image in their minds or make a connection with the name — it remains abstract to them. Similarly, people who tend to be right-brained can find it difficult to read, because words are abstract to them. When you are finding a lot of things abstract, you may find yourself falling behind in conversation or struggling to follow a presentation or a meeting, because your mind is playing catch-up, trying to decode all the information it is receiving.

Just as Confucius said 'I hear and I forget', if you are unable to decode the message quickly enough, you will indeed forget. So the next step is to be able to 'see'.

2 IMAGE
(I see and I remember)

To make things more memorable, we need to convert the abstract into an image. This process allows us to move from using our left brain to using the right. As the saying goes, 'A picture is worth a thousand words'. An image can convey complex ideas quickly.

With simple information, our minds may easily form an image. For example, when someone says 'elephant' to you, you may see an elephant in your mind. Our minds are already trained to form images. But some information is a lot harder to turn into an image. Consider how much easier it will be to remember my name (Tansel) if you picture tinsel in your mind. You have an image to recall now!

To understand how useful and important images can be in communication, imagine a busy city street with many street signs. Most of the signs use symbols (images). Any words on signs are generally kept very short: 'STOP' or 'GO'. What would happen if all the street signs were written in sentences instead? It would take drivers much longer to process the messages, and by the time they did another sign would have popped up, and another. This would cause confusion and possibly lead to car accidents. The brain processes images much more quickly. An image represents a piece of information that can be easily understood just by looking at it.

Of course, it also helps to make the image as bright and unusual as possible. That is why I called this model the Yellow Elephant: a yellow elephant is a much more memorable image than a grey one!

3 ASSOCIATION
(I do and I understand)

Association is the key ingredient to remembering. It is best done by using your imagination to make a story. Sometimes forming an image is not enough. There needs to be a *connection* so that the basis of remembering is formed. Connection means the left and right sides of the brain work together, which is how you develop amazing memory and recall. Most of the time, if not all, you have more than one thing to remember. Hence, connection has to occur between all the elements in order for them to be remembered. The process of association allows this to occur through linking information. Using your imagination to make a story is the best way to initiate this.

When you do something active with an image in your head, forming a story with it, you are far more likely to actively remember and understand it. The brain can't determine what is real and what is imagined, so if you make up stories involving action, it is almost like you have 'done' that particular action, resulting in understanding or some sort of competence. For example, I love playing tennis, but I don't get to play much due to my busy lifestyle. So, I practise hitting shots in my head. I visualise how I should hold the racquet and toss the ball when serving. I even simulate in my mind how my opponent would move to try and catch me out. I've been doing this ever since I was a child, when I played just about every sport at school. One year I did not play tennis at all, and when I came back I was hopeless. I started practising quite heavily in my head and got better in the following weeks, eventually beating everyone at the club — something I thought was impossible because of the calibre of the players I played against.

This association step can be used for all sorts of purposes. I now use it to prepare for my keynote speeches and training. I visualise and make up in my mind the 'story' of the day and how

I will present. This also helps me considerably to make accurate judgements about how much time each section of a talk will take. I make sure to memorise links between sections of a talk — for instance between the introduction and a memory test for the audience. I visualise the audience's reactions and imagine saying the words, 'I've done my memorisation part, but since you're here for a memory session, let's test *your* memory as well.'

4 COMMUNICATION

You've made it memorable for yourself, now how about for others? You have the story in your head, but now you need to transfer what you have in your head to the rest of the world. Unfortunately, this is not as easy as it seems.

I'm sure at some point in your life you've experienced a 'Death by PowerPoint' presentation — a presentation where the slides are crowded with lots of text and the presenter spends the whole time reading them out verbatim. It's very difficult for an audience to engage with this sort of presentation. Unfortunately, people mostly use their left brain for study and work, so it becomes 'natural' to use this side when they want to present information. That's why they might use so many words, all in one colour and with a boring structure, even when they are using a visual medium such as PowerPoint. It's unfortunate, because PowerPoint was never designed to be used that way.

If people are only reading words from a slide and trying to listen to a presenter, they may not even progress beyond step 1 — abstract. They will understand some parts of the presentation, of course, but most people will become disengaged after a while and not take anything in. The people who fully understand the presentation will be creating images in their minds, as in step 2. However, there is a chance they may not be able to put their learning into context, as the point on the slide or even the slide itself may have passed by too quickly.

To communicate and get our message across effectively and engage the audience, we need to use both sides of our brain. Communication is all about passing on our message in the best possible way — and the best possible way to use your brain is to use both sides.

Tips for Using The Yellow Elephant Model

- Practise creating images for non-concrete words such as 'hibernation' (for example, a bear in a den) or 'creativity' (perhaps coloured pencils). For detailed visualisation techniques see 'Memory Techniques'.
- Make sure you make strong connections when you are making a story. A pen *near* the computer is not a strong association, but a pen *writing on* a computer is. An even better association is a pen *breaking through* the computer.
- Negativity works better than positivity when making stories. Just look at the news reports on television: they are almost all negative. Television news crews know how to make 'drama' that is memorable and evokes emotion. A family having dinner and talking about everyday life may not be an exciting story, but if one of the kids threw an apple at the dad and knocked him out, that creates drama.

Memory Techniques

'It is lovely, when I forget all birthdays, including my own, to find that somebody remembers me.'

— ELLEN GLASGOW

PEOPLE HAVE ASKED ME why I memorise numbers and playing cards and do memory training. In response, I ask them why people play sport or go jogging. They usually answer something like 'to get fit' or 'to stay healthy'. Then I ask what people do to get their brain fit. The answer almost all the time is 'nothing'. Some people have even said to me that with all the memorising I do I must have no life. Just imagine if I said that to someone who was at the gym working out! 'You're doing a bench press? Pfft, you have no life!' The fact is that memory training is a skill to keep our minds fit — as well as a lot of fun.

Memory training is the ultimate brain training. Crossword puzzles, mobile apps and mind games are all useful, but they provide nowhere near the strength that memory training does. Memory training works the core of your imagination, and creativity is a quicker way to train both sides of your brain.

If you want to keep mentally fit, train your memory. The techniques in this chapter will get you started.

The Linking Techniques

One of the simplest memory techniques is linking. Let's say you have a shopping list of five items. You link those items together in an imaginative and memorable story. For example, let's say we want to buy the following items: tomatoes, carrots, eggs, chocolate chip biscuits and vegetable soup. To remember these items using the link system, we could make up the following story:

> You walk into supermarket and see everyone dressed as TOMATOES bouncing around the store. The manager of the supermarket finds you and asks you what's wrong, as if you're an alien, unfamiliar to their tomato race. He cannot comprehend what you are saying, so he sticks a CARROT in your ear. This carrot then starts to grow inside your ear and lifts you up like a balloon and flies you crazily around the supermarket. Finally, you somehow manage to pop the carrot out of your ear while still up in the air, but you suddenly fall down into a huge basket of EGGS. (I'm sure you can imagine what a mess that would make!) You pick yourself up, deciding that you've had enough of this supermarket. You want to make a quick exit and head for the door, when all of a sudden: bang! A giant BISCUIT covers the exit and you smash your head on the chocolate chips.
>
> You remain unconscious until one of the tomato dudes pours very hot VEGETABLE SOUP all over you and you wake up *tasting, smelling* and even *looking* like soup.

Now close the book and see if you can recall the shopping list items.

As you might have noticed, the crazier and funnier you make your story, the easier it is to remember. To further increase your chances of remembering the story, use all your senses — taste, touch, smell, sound — as well. Did you notice how the feeling of messy, broken eggs, or the smell or taste of soup was very vivid in the story above?

Memorise the ten items below using the link system.

1. Coffee
2. Cucumber
3. Honey
4. Toilet Paper
5. Bread
6. Milk
7. Rice
8. Chocolate
9. Yoghurt
10. Pumpkin

The VAI Memory Principle

The VAI memory principle allows the memorisation process to become much stronger, so recall is a lot easier. VAI stands for visualisation, association, imagination.

If memorisation is not initially successful people go back and repeat the process, trying to better remember the information. However, as we have seen, repetition is not the best way to remember, as it can become stressful, monotonous and a waste of time. Repetition can simply be doing step 1 — abstract over and over, which means you may not even reach the image or association part of the Yellow Elephant model.

Visualisation

When we picture something, we generally see a *static* image of it. For example, if I say the word 'whiteboard', most people would visualise a whiteboard on a wall or a portable whiteboard in a classroom or lecture room they are familiar with. Or if someone says 'chair', you may picture a standard wooden dining room chair. This image does not move. It is just a visual of what you see in your mind's eye.

Memory is all about imagination. Imagination can take something ordinary and make it weird, funny, exciting and way beyond the 'norm'. Imagination is one of the most powerful things we possess as a human being.

So, if you visualise something that is static, boring and not moving, use your imagination to make it stick in your head: for example, imagine the whiteboard, in different colours, spinning around and singing you a song in the process. While this may seem silly and not something that's going to happen in real life, it will prompt your brain to remember what that spinning crazy thing was — the whiteboard. The sillier and more outlandish the visualisation, the better it will stick in your mind. If your visualisation makes no sense, your brain will question it, saying 'this doesn't make sense'. The fact that the brain is asking why indicates mental engagement. If you are asking yourself questions, you are involving yourself. The more involvement you have, more chances are that the visualisation you make will be imaginative, ensuring you will remember it.

Visualisation Skills Test
Below are words to test your visualisation skills. Next to each word, write down how you creatively visualise the word.

1. hammer

_____

2. eggplant

_____

3. noise

_____

4. apple

_____

5. craft

_____

6. tree

_____

7. drink

_____

8. baby

_____

9. white

_____

10. player

_____

11. giraffe

_____

12. computer

_____

13. smelly

_____

14. shine

_____

15. silk

_____

16. memory

_____

17. tooth

_____

18. state

19. embarrassed

20. sleuth

How did you do? Some of them would have been very easy, whereas some were probably more difficult. For example, there is no obvious visual for the word 'memory' because it is not a concrete object. However, we may associate the word 'memory' with things such as 'forgetting', 'brain' or 'RAM'. This should allow us to find an image that will act as a memory trigger for the word 'memory'.

Association

You have your visualisation all worked out — now it's time to connect. As we saw in the Yellow Elephant model, association is the main driver for remembering things. It is the process of linking one thing to another. If there is no association, then there is very weak memory. Strong association provides instant recall. The main reason I was able to memorise the phonebook was because I focused on getting the association right.

So, what is association? Association is developing a strong story with two or more items of data connected together.

The trick to association is linking items to be memorised together physically in your mind. 'I walked past the dog' is not a very strong association. Nor is 'I stood near the car'. Both these examples have no physical link between me and the object (dog or car). 'I hugged the dog', 'I caressed the dog', maybe even 'I licked the dog' … these are much more interesting! Especially the latter, as it engages your senses and is a bit gross for most people. Notice how I connected myself physically to the subject.

Now let's take the example of the car. I could use 'I accidently scratched the car' or 'I fell on top of the bonnet'. I could also visualise being inside the car. If you can visualise a car well and it interests you, the association will work. However, something that is 'logical', such as hopping into a car, represents an everyday occurrence (in this case, driving a vehicle). Because it is such a normal occurrence, it may not engage your brain very much, as you are used to seeing this visual representation. Use your imagination to think of something more inventive.

Below are some words with which to practise forming associations. Always make sure you first visualise the words, making them stand out in your mind. Then exercise your imagination by linking the two words together.

Write down your association story in the space under the words.

1. ice-cream — horse

_____

2. star — spray

_____

3. keyboard — leaf

_____

4. book — mouse

_____

5. flag — scream

_____

6. guitar — pencil

_____

7. egg — freaky

_____

8. summer — lightweight

_____

9. silly — hypothetical

_____

10. experience — mediation

_____

11. Lamborghini — cradle

_____

12. swimmer — theory

_____

13. sprout — agile

_____

14. cream — absorb

_____

15. fishing — camel

_____

16. sweat — picnic

_____

17. adaptation — relative

_____

18. creative — hibernation

---

19. shallow — rhythm

---

20. deal — torrential

You probably found that making associations between two particularly abstract words (for example 'deal' and 'torrential') is difficult. This is what we are faced with in our daily lives. Things aren't always presented to us easily. We are confronted with situations where we are forced to think and act quickly, which can result in stress, embarrassment, indecision and so on. If you don't exercise your capability to think, then you are limiting your ability to contribute. The best way to build association skills is to practise. Chapter on brain training ('Ultimate Brain Training') will show you how you can practise and work on those imagination muscles.

Imagination

When I first get people to make up stories using their imagination, they usually start thinking of things that make logical sense in this world. For example, if I said the word 'chair', they would imagine someone sitting on a chair, or perhaps sitting on a chair themselves — because that's essentially what you do with a chair.

However, imagination can break all the rules. It has no barriers. Instead of imagining standard everyday images and action, try something different that cannot possibly be done in this world. For example: 'you tried to sit on the chair, it turned around and said "No, thanks" and walked off, as it didn't want your butt sitting on it.' Yes, it's silly, but the sillier the image, the simpler it is to recall. This is one of the reasons why cartoons are so popular: they exercise imagination through amazing creativity. Who in real life runs past the edge of a cliff, suddenly realises they are suspended in mid-air and then quickly hurries back to safety?

You want to be able to create a whole new world filled with awesome imaginative stories so that you can eventually bring it back down to 'earth' level. What I mean by this is, instead of having one or two ideas in a board meeting, you might now have ten or eleven due to the quick workings of your brain. Bringing out your imaginary world into the real world is how you think outside the square. If you want to think outside the square, or even way beyond it, exercise your imagination!

There is just one thing to be careful with when using the VAI principle. If you get very skilled at using it, be wary of visualising negative events, such as a relationship break-up or an embarrassing workplace moment, as the VAI principle can amplify them as well. If that happens, it is best to disassociate from the story by imagining it all turning grey in colour and disappearing into the far distance. This takes some of the emotional charge out of the scenario in your head. You can also use the VAI principle to accentuate better moments so you can focus on them instead.

Method of Loci

So how can we use both sides of our brain to remember? The Method of Loci is one way to do so. Thousands of years ago, the Ancient Greeks used a technique called the Method of Loci to memorise large amounts of information. They did this by walking through a familiar path and attaching items they wanted to remember to landmarks along the way.

Picture this. Let's say Craigimidis decides to memorise a shopping list. He walks out of his house and the first thing he sees are two goats staring at him, bleating 'maaa'. So he chooses the two goats as his first location, or *locus*. He walks further and sees his neighbour's house. 'Good morning, Socrates,' says Craigimidis. He mentally notes down his neighbour's house as his second *locus*. Walking further on, he sees a really large tree — third *locus,* followed by a broken-down fence beside it — fourth *locus*. He climbs over the broken fence to enter the town centre. It's all hustle and bustle. The first thing he sees there is a statue of the late, great twelve-time winner of the Ancient Greek Memory Championships, Kevin O'Brienus, and he makes that his fifth *locus*.

Craigimidis has now chosen landmarks along a familiar journey, in the sequence he would see them during his short walk. Hence, his journey looks like this:

1. two goats
2. neighbour's house
3. large tree
4. broken-down fence
5. Kevin O'Brienus statue

Now, all Craigimidis has to do is attach what he wants to remember to the locations *(loci)* along his journey. For example, if his shopping list consisted of cucumber, bread, fish, soap and flowers, he would structure his ideas like this:

	Item to be memorised	*Locus*
1.	cucumber	two goats
2.	bread	neighbour's house
3.	fish	large tree
4.	soap	broken-down fence
5.	flowers	Kevin O'Brienus statue

He would link the words to the *loci* using association skills:

1. You feed a ten-foot long cucumber to the two goats.
2. You make nice fresh bread with your own hands and throw it into your neighbour's house. It ends up on their kitchen bench. Good throw!
3. There are fish growing on the large tree. You pick one off and put it over your shoulder, as it weighs 20 kg.
4. You decide to fix the broken fence with a bar of soap.
5. Flowers surround the Kevin statue. You buy a bunch and lay them down as a sign of respect.

Close the book and try to recall these stories, one by one, then fill in the item associated with each *locus* below.

1. two goats

_____

2. neighbour's house

_____

3. large tree

_____

4. broken-down fence

_____

5. Kevin O'Brienus statue

_____

The benefit of the Method of Loci is that you can have as many locations as you want. This means you can remember large amounts of information. The best place to start developing a Method of Loci is around your home. You know your home very well and can mentally navigate through it quite easily. Below is an example of locations in a house that can be used for the Method of Loci.

Room 1 Bedroom	Room 2 Living room	Room 3 Bathroom	Room 4 Study	Room 5 Backyard
1. Bed	6. Couch	11. Toilet	16. Computer	21. Patio
2. Window	7. TV	12. Shower	17. Bookshelf	22. Flowers
3. Cupboard	8. Coffee table	13. Sink	18. Table	23. Shed
4. Drawers	9. Vase	14. Towel rack	19. Window	24. Trampoline
5. Wardrobe	10. Painting	15. Mirror	20. Guitar	25. Lemon tree

This make-believe house has twenty-five locations. You can attach items to be remembered to each location. If you want to remember twenty-five items, you can attach one item to each location.

Now for the cool part: you are not restricted to adding only one item to a location. You can add as many as you like. So, if you wanted to remember fifty words, you could add two words to each location. If you had a hundred words to remember, there would be four words to a location. Your recall success will be determined by how well you come up with stories.

'Application of Techniques' demonstrates various applications for the Method of Loci.

The Peg Words Technique (Major System*)

Without any technique, numbers — whether they be telephone numbers, anniversary dates, PIN numbers or product codes — are very difficult to remember. However, I memorised over

---

* The words technique and system are interchangeable.

twenty thousand digits in eighteen days. If I hadn't used a technique and instead just repeated them *ad nauseum,* I would not have remembered more than seven or eight digits.

Have you ever forgotten an important birthday or anniversary? Or perhaps you've been at the checkout and forgotten your PIN. How did you feel? It can be embarrassing.

The Major system provides a great way to memorise numbers. In the Major system, you create peg words. Peg words are words used to replace numbers so that they can act as conceptual hooks. Onto these hooks, we can hang, or attach, items in a list. With some practise, this approach makes memorising numbers a piece of cake. It may seem confusing at first, but don't despair: it gets easier and easier the more you use it.

The Major system uses the phonetic sounds of the alphabet for each digit. When you substitute the digits with the sounds, you can then create a peg word. For example, by substituting the digit 1 with a 'd', and the digit 7 with a 'k', you would have a 'd' and a 'k' to represent the number 17. We don't stop here. Since there are only ten different digits — 0, 1, 2, 3, 4, 5 6, 7, 8 and 9 — and there are twenty-six letters in the alphabet, the creators of the Major system left some spare letters for us to use when we create peg words! The spare letters are all the vowels — 'a', 'e', 'i', 'o', 'u' — and 'h', 'w' and 'y'. When forming peg words, you can select any of the spare characters to insert before, between or after the substitute letter(s). In the case of number 17, your peg word could be the word 'duck' ('ck' makes the same sound as a 'k' when it is spoken).

Below is a breakdown of the numbers and their corresponding sounds.

0	S, Z, soft C (e.g. ceiling)
1	T or D
2	N
3	M
4	R
5	L
6	J, SH, CH, soft G (e.g. Germany) DG (e.g. nudge)
7	K, CK, hard C (e.g. cat), hard G (e.g. goat), hard CH (e.g. chorus) QU (e.g. grotesque)
8	V or F
9	B or P

Using the information above, you can make a hundred peg words, from 0 to 99. For example, as a peg word for the number 1 you could have: 'tea', 'toe', 'hat' or 'at'. Number 2 could be 'Noah', 'in' or 'one'. Play around with different combinations of numbers and see if you can make up words for them.

On the next page is a table of ninety-nine peg words I have come up with. Check how these words correspond with the above numbers. You are welcome to use this table or make up your own peg words.

0 = saw	20 = nose	40 = rose	60 = cheese	80 = vase
1 = hat	21 = wand	41 = rat	61 = chat	81 = fat
2 = hen	22 = nun	42 = Arnie	62 = chain	82 = van
3 = ham	23 = gnome	43 = arm	63 = chime	83 = fame
4 = hair	24 = Nero	44 = roar	64 = chair	84 = fur
5 = hail	25 = nail	45 = rail	65 = jelly	85 = veal
6 = hatch	26 = nudge	46 = rash	66 = cha-cha	86 = fish
7 = hack	27 = Nike	47 = rock	67 = choc	87 = fog
8 = hoof	28 = knife	48 = reef	68 = chef	88 = fife
9 = hoop	29 = nappy	49 = ruby	69 = ship	89 = fab
10 = doze	30 = mouse	50 = loose	70 = Agassi	90 = bass
11 = dot	31 = mad	51 = wallet	71 = cat	91 = bat
12 = dine	32 = money	52 = alien	72 = gun	92 = pen
13 = dome	33 = ma'am	53 = limo	73 = comb	93 = bam
14 = door	34 = Homer	54 = lawyer	74 = car	94 = pear
15 = dale	35 = mail	55 = lily	75 = glue	95 = pale
16 = DJ	36 = MJ	56 = leech	76 = couch	96 = peach
17 = duck	37 = Maccas	57 = leg	77 = cake	97 = bike
18 = Daffy	38 = mafia	58 = love	78 = coffee	98 = beef
19 = tape	39 = map	59 = elbow	79 = cab	99 = babe

Take some time to memorise and familiarise yourself with these peg words or the set of peg words you make up yourself. Start by memorising ten at a time at your own pace. Write down your peg words on paper, then test yourself. For starters, I recommend going through the numbers slowly, at a speed you are comfortable with, so you have enough time to recall the peg word.

Once you engrave these peg words into your head, you will be armed with a powerful memorisation tool!

So, how would you memorise the number 714277? Begin by pairing up the digits to get 71 42 77. Then all you have to do is remember what your peg words for those numbers are and make up a creative little story using them. For example: 71 = cat, 42 = Arnie (Arnold Schwarzenegger), and 77 = cake. So the story could be something like this. 'the CAT jumps into ARNIE's birthday CAKE as he is about to blow out the candles, creating a huge mess'. This story is much more memorable than boring 714277, isn't it? We have now associated images and incorporated our senses to make a number a memorable thing!

Once you have practised memorising numbers in pairs, you can also try making up peg words three digits at a time. If we use the same example as above, we'd have 714 277. 714 = gator, 214 = enter. The story could be: 'the alliGATOR sprung out of the lake and started to fly towards the do not ENTER sign, eating and ripping the rusty sign into shreds'. Since when did alligators fly? In your mind, anything can fly. Use your imagination to make really wild and whacky stories. They don't have to make sense, as long as you link the peg words together and the story is memorable to you. Using humour and drawing in each of your senses makes the memorisation even stronger and helps you to recall more quickly.

This method works well when trying to memorise short numbers of ten to twenty digits. After that, people commonly have a problem trying to remember the order in which they memorised the pairs of numbers. One way to beat this issue is to use the Method of Loci (see page 33). Since your journey is ordered, you can simply associate each pair or triplet of digits with a stop in your journey. For example, using the number 873874522240, we would begin by pairing up the numbers: 87, 38, 74, 52, 22 and 40. Using the *loci* from the table on page

34 finish off the journey and you will find that long digits are actually hard to forget! Techniques such as this one have been used by participants at World Memory Championships to achieve outstanding results. People have memorized hundreds, even thousands of digits in a matter of minutes using this technique.

The journey begins with the **bed,** which is made out of FOG! People try to sit on it but helplessly fall onto the ground instead. So they change their minds and walk over to the **window,** where they are greeted by friendly members of the MAFIA wearing white aprons over their classy black suits while they cook up delicious meals for the people with sore backsides. After eating, the mafia members run into a **cupboard,** where they have parked their CAR. They get in and drive away, but lose control of their car and crash into the set of **drawers** that were full of little green ALIENS. You freak out and start to run away but end up walking straight into a **wardrobe.** It's very dark inside so you flick the light switch and find a NUN standing right beside you, smiling. You receive quite a scare and jump out of your skin and land on the **couch,** bouncing up and down. As you do so you hear a screeching sound. It's a CAT!

Practise memorizing the numbers on the following pages. With the first page of numbers, pair them up. Then use groups of three digits for the second page of numbers. While it may seem daunting, with a bit of practice at creating images and building them into stories, you will find that it gets easier. You will find that using the Method of Loci works best for longer numbers. In no time you will be able to memorise a whole row of forty digits.

30884406674522970121809672326302104068 39

73979548512602844491909738293135084313 08

85479828309752327285541872261878686624 84

96106644874853936630531303615714528283 98

50369689209619285728165871491037714999 08

5919573976482687795376816157814152504383

09353805794821366682928052647141548813 81

01280429309913131082349915094268773306 01

51133253292262396480973237143978601121 46

78838558454278906167194664162996775148 90

98142376640058598780137675536357951783 13

83228223397398191843092487705224196380 09

82415116537064948620099861072078585805 72

22838161288155287259139885039756290692 88

14111026199310896915121041574178516160 68

69615011199955539890070497842899270136 68

11861745381676151509276977364339074292 25

80454313857617689143960690375305514946 92

79135794017461104316009457324158234703 88

11765499709420655445404478997296889036 71

94927386084199167084398982992344053162 69

87361850773422678617240117105555941156 94

0 6 1 4 9 7 5 1 9 3 7 5 1 8 2 3 0 8 3 1 8 5 7 8 2 1 9 3 2 5 0 1 1 1 3 2 9 6 1 2

0 9 6 6 7 2 3 8 1 0 9 6 1 6 2 4 8 5 7 6 9 8 2 7 3 2 6 5 7 5 6 8 5 5 5 8 7 9 0 5

7 6 8 3 7 3 8 0 1 2 0 7 3 6 3 3 2 6 8 3 7 0 9 7 4 0 2 5 7 9 5 9 2 0 2 7 2 3 2 7

4 0 9 3 8 6 7 6 3 5 4 9 0 0 0 0 9 6 6 8 5 1 6 3 7 6 1 7 4 7 8 8 1 6 6 8 2 1 6 2

6 6 4 2 4 1 9 8 2 4 4 2 3 4 4 6 1 1 8 8 5 1 4 4 2 4 7 9 6 0 0 8 5 2 2 9 7 5 8 0

1 5 0 2 3 6 0 7 5 0 4 8 5 0 4 9 7 2 8 2 3 8 1 8 6 7 8 8 1 2 0 2 8 0 8 8 9 5 7 5

9 4 4 8 3 6 5 2 5 5 4 8 7 9 9 9 0 1 0 7 3 0 6 1 6 4 3 9 4 7 5 0 5 3 8 5 7 2 1 0

9 8 7 4 4 1 8 2 3 5 8 8 2 5 4 2 8 7 9 1 2 8 9 6 1 8 3 5 4 9 5 8 2 1 9 3 3 4 1 7

3 7 8 5 3 6 0 5 6 7 2 9 6 5 8 3 5 4 5 8 9 7 5 6 8 0 7 0 8 0 4 7 6 3 1 6 8 4 9 8

6 2 9 2 2 5 9 1 0 2 5 5 9 5 1 6 8 8 9 2 1 8 4 1 4 4 4 2 8 0 1 3 4 4 8 5 1 6 1 1

5 1 1 5 5 3 5 3 6 1 8 5 5 7 0 2 4 5 9 8 8 5 9 3 2 1 4 2 2 7 3 2 8 7 9 0 2 0 0 9

4 4 3 9 7 0 8 5 5 8 4 8 9 9 5 1 0 9 5 0 8 7 1 7 5 0 1 7 4 9 3 6 2 0 7 0 6 7 6 5

0 6 3 9 2 7 7 5 2 7 5 3 5 4 7 2 6 1 6 3 6 9 7 4 9 9 9 3 6 1 9 6 4 6 6 4 0 6 0 5

1 8 7 4 4 9 7 4 3 3 1 6 5 4 4 4 1 1 2 9 2 2 0 5 7 4 2 5 0 1 0 8 1 0 9 6 6 7 2 2

0 3 4 0 2 3 5 5 3 3 4 4 5 3 3 3 9 2 5 2 7 9 9 5 2 6 8 9 5 5 0 0 4 4 9 9 7 8 5 4

3 3 5 3 4 5 1 1 4 8 8 0 6 4 4 0 9 0 3 9 7 8 0 8 4 5 9 1 4 3 7 9 8 8 8 0 5 3 0 1

0 0 6 3 0 8 1 3 2 9 8 1 5 4 1 3 2 7 6 3 5 6 4 0 1 9 5 6 6 7 4 5 2 7 2 3 0 4 4 1

1 2 7 5 2 7 4 9 0 7 2 5 4 8 5 1 4 5 1 3 6 6 2 4 0 1 9 6 5 2 4 9 9 2 5 7 2 1 7 0

2 1 6 4 1 9 5 7 3 8 1 2 1 7 4 8 0 2 2 3 0 7 0 7 6 1 7 7 3 3 5 9 9 1 8 3 2 8 3 4

4 0 5 7 1 9 4 8 8 9 4 5 2 2 9 7 6 9 3 4 8 0 4 4 3 3 0 3 6 4 3 0 6 2 8 0 6 3 1 9

6 0 2 4 1 1 4 9 0 6 5 1 2 3 3 3 5 4 1 1 3 7 6 0 0 3 9 4 0 6 2 5 4 2 2 7 3 9 1 4

9 7 3 6 7 5 3 3 7 3 6 0 1 6 3 8 5 2 0 7 2 2 0 1 0 2 9 2 2 5 1 7 0 2 7 5 8 5 3 3

Person/Action (PA) System

The PA system allows you to memorise numbers by developing a story based on individual people and their associated actions. Here's how it works:

1. Assign a person to each number from 0 to 99, using the Major system. For example, 17 could be Tiger (1 = T and 7 = G), which could represent Tiger Woods. The number 42 could be Arnie (4 = R and 2 = N): Arnold Schwarzenegger.

2. Assign an action for each person from 0 to 99. The action for Tiger Woods could be 'swinging' a golf club. For Arnold Schwarzenegger, it could be 'lifting' weights.

3. The first two digits will now represent a person and the next two digits will represent the action. For example, if we take 1742, the 17 will be the person (Tiger Woods) and 42 the action for Arnold Schwarzenegger (lifting). So to remember 1742, the story would be 'Tiger Woods is lifting'. Let's try another: 9463 (94 = Bart from *The Simpsons,* 63 = Jimmy Hendrix, with the action 'strumming' his guitar). So, the story for 9463 is 'Bart Simpson is strumming'. Now you're probably thinking: 'Tiger Woods is lifting what?' Or 'Bart Simpson is strumming what?' The story is not yet quite finished. It needs to be merged with a *locus* to ensure you remember the numbers in the correct sequence. Stories with a person, an action and a *locus* are short and practical to remember, so to remember long digits of numbers in order, use *loci*. We've given an example on the next page, using the *loci* from the table on page 34. See if you can fill in the rest with your whacky stories.

1. Bed   9463 (Bart Simpson is strumming on my **bed.**)
2. Window   1742 (Tiger Woods is lifting my **window.**)
3. Cupboard 8654 _____

                    _____

4. Drawer   1098 _____

                    _____

5. Wardrobe 2119 _____

                    _____

Person/Action/Object (PAO) System

The PAO system is the same as the PA system, but with another set of images for a specified object for numbers 0 to 99. This means every person with an action also has an associated object. If we use the same image examples as above, then 174217 will be Tiger Woods (person), lifting (action) and his golf club (object). Golf club becomes the object for 17 (Tiger Woods). Similarly, the object for 42, Arnold Schwarzenegger, could be weights.

Have a go at memorising the following sets of numbers using the PAO system.

```
227732  405912  432598  530263  065267  779096
010580  496884  814019  362197  642871  442741
917122  812222  452853  449535  323231  688997
607269  706329  603220  750976  782120  389146
153338  335955  677439  782899  430000  084828
303127  523105  492339  634171  715052  999541
164173  893142  571526  689571  880342  620596
322546  374716  176301  343882  203081  002779
```

Active Loci Integration (ALI) Method

Creating location for the Method of Loci and then remembering them really well can sometimes be a tedious process. Also, if you've just memorised something to your set of *loci*, you generally have to wait a while, usually a few days or so, to memorise something else using this same *loci*, or you will get mixed up with what you've previously memorised. If you're like me and don't necessarily want to create thousands of *loci*, then the Active Loci Integration (ALI) method is the answer.

The ALI method is a *loci*-based system for memorising that can be reused immediately, because unlike the Method of Loci, it uses a limited set of locations, just like peg words.

Here's how it works.

For every image (peg word) you have per number or playing card, you have an associated location. For example, using the Major system, the number 92 can equal 'pen'. To create a *locus* for 'pen' we need to think 'where can we find a pen?' This is where you can add your own personal association for the pen *locus*.

Since pens can be bought at stationery shops, I made my *locus* Office works. Here are some examples for memorising numbers:

34 = Homer (from *The Simpsons*), *locus*: the Simpsons' house
47 = Rocky (Balboa), *locus*: boxing ring
98 = beef, *locus*: butcher

and for memorising playing cards:

KS = spade, *locus*: gardening shop
7D = dog, *locus*: kennel
4C = car, *locus*: garage

Below is a chart you can use if you choose.

No.	Image	Locus	No.	Image	Locus
0	sauce	pantry	1	seat	inside car
2	sun	sky	3	sumo	sumo ring
4	sir	lectern	5	sell	pawnbroker
6	sash	contest	7	sock	drawer
8	safe	bank	9	soap	sink
10	doze	bed	11	dot	wall
12	dine	dinner table	13	dome	mosque
14	door	house	15	dale	mountains
16	DJ	nightclub	17	duck	pond
18	Daffy	woods	19	tape	pencil case
20	nose	face	21	wand	fairy's hand
22	nun	convent	23	gnome	front yard
24	Nero	Rome	25	nail	nail gun
26	nudge	elbow	27	Nike	shoe
28	knife	kitchen	29	nappy	baby
30	mouse	wheel	31	mad	magazine
32	moon	space	33	ma'am	diner
34	Homer	Simpsons' house	35	mail	post office
36	MJ	Neverland	37	mic	on stage
38	mafia	mansion	39	map	gps unit
40	rose	field	41	rat	basement
42	Arnie	gym	43	arm	plaster cast
44	roar	lion's den	45	rail	train station
46	rash	arm	47	Rock	ringside
48	roof	on top of house	49	ruby	underground
50	lace	shoe	51	wallet	pocket
52	alien	spaceship	53	limo	hire company
54	lawyer	courtroom	55	lily	field
56	leech	swamp	57	leg	body
58	leaf	tree	59	leap	sandpit

60	cheese	supermarket	61	chat	computer
62	chain	bike shop	63	chime	door
64	chair	computer desk	65	jelly	fridge
66	cha-cha	dance floor	67	choc	candy store
68	chef	kitchen	69	ship	dock
70	Agassi	tennis court	71	cat	cat bed
72	gun	holster	73	comb	in afro
74	car	garage	75	glue	classroom
76	cash	bank	77	cake	bakery
78	coffee	café	79	cab	taxi rank
80	vase	shelf	81	fat	restaurant
82	fan	rock concert	83	fame	movie set
84	fur	dead animal	85	veal	schnitzel
86	fish	sea	87	fog	road
88	fife	music store	89	Fab	laundry
90	bass	guitar amp	91	bat	tree
92	pen	pen holder	93	bam	fighting ring
94	pear	grocery store	95	pale	hospital
96	peace	protest	97	bike	bike track
98	beef	bbq	99	babe	podium

Playing Cards

AS	seat	airplane	AH	hat	hat stand
2S	sun	Milky Way	2H	honey	beehive
3S	sumo	sumo ring	3H	Homer	Simpsons' house
4S	sir	lectern	4H	hair	hairdresser
5S	sell	pawnbroker	5H	hail	sky
6S	sash	contest	6H	hash	hash brown
7S	sock	drawer	7H	hack	computer
8S	safe	bank	8H	hoof	horse
9S	soap	bathroom	9H	hoop	circle
10S	sauce	pantry	10H	hose	garden
JS	sited	telescope	JH	hated	war

QS	Satan	hell	QH	heathen	village
KS	spade	vegie garden	KH	heart	inside body
AD	day	calendar	AC	cat	cat bed
2D	tan	beach	2C	gun	holster
3D	dome	mosque	3C	comb	in afro
4D	door	house	4C	car	garage
5D	doll	dollhouse	5C	glue	classroom
6D	DJ	nightclub	6C	cash	bank
7D	duck	pond	7C	cake	pastry shop
8D	Daffy	woods	8C	coffee	café
9D	tape	pencil case	9C	cab	taxi rank
10D	doze	bed	10C	Agassi	tennis court
JD	dotted	line	JC	kitted	ute
QD	Daytona	international speedway	QC	kitten	in arms
KD	diamond	mine	KC	club	baseball pitch

To memorise using the ALI method, you start with an initial *locus*, then you link the images and *loci* in a sequence. For example, if you had the numbers 9247328876 to memorise, you would:

1. Select an initial *locus*: couch (this only occurs once).

2. Link the image for 92 (pen) to couch: 'The PEN was writing on the **couch**'.

3. Link the image for 47 (Rock) to the *locus* of 92 (pen holder): 'The ROCK did a body slam on my **pen holder**'.

4. Link the image for 32 (moon) to the *locus* of 47 (ringside): 'The MOON landed **ringside** to watch the wrestling match'.

5. Link the image for 88 (fife) to the *locus* of 32 (space): 'I was playing the FIFE very loud out in **space**'.

6. Finally, link the image for 76 (cash) to the *locus* of 88 (band): 'I presented CASH to the **band** so they would stop playing horrible music'.

Here's an example of how to use the ALI method to memorise the following playing cards: 2 of Spades, 10 of Hearts, King of Diamonds, 3 of Clubs, 6 of Diamonds.

1. Select an initial *locus*: toilet.

2. Link the image for 2 of Spades (sun) to toilet: 'The SUN was shining heavily on the **toilet** seat'.

3. Now link the image for 10 of Hearts (hose) to the *locus* of 2 of Spades (sky): 'I lifted the HOSE into the **sky** and turned the tap on full'.

4. Now link the image for King of Diamonds (diamond) to the *locus* of 10 of Hearts (garden): 'I found a ten-foot DIAMOND in the **garden**'.

5. Link the image for 3 of Clubs (comb) to the *locus* of King of Diamonds (mine): 'Everyone had to COMB their hair before they entered **mine**, for occupational health and safety reasons'.

6. Finally, link the image for 6 of Diamonds (DJ) to the *locus* of 3 of Clubs (in afro): 'The DJ had a huge **afro** hairstyle and was playing disco funk music'.

The ALI method has several benefits over a static *loci* method:

- The *locus* of the number or card before the next item to be memorised acts as a memory prompt for that particular image.
- You can memorise using the same system over and over again, without having to wait a few days to make sure you don't confuse it with what you memorised previously. I call this 'memory overlap'.
- You do not have to create new locations. You just need to link the existing ones to the cards or numbers.
- You can use the PA and PAO systems with the ALI method to memorise more numbers and cards. This is great for mental athletes competing in memory championships.

Helpful Hints

Here are some helpful hints for using the ALI method:

- ☑ Make sure you make your locations, as well as your images, memorable.
- ☑ Practice makes perfect. Keep at it!
- ☑ Try out different images and loci and find out what is most memorable for you.
- ☑ Start slowly when you first begin. It can be difficult trying to link a *locus* to the next number or card without getting mixed up with the previous one. Once you have mastered this, you can go a lot faster.
- ☑ Take your time. There is no rush. The more time you take to develop your stories, attaching them to the *loci*, the stronger your recall will be.

Key Points

- Once you've understood how the techniques work, you'll be able to remember just about anything. Try using the Method of Loci to remember poetry, speeches, sporting statistics … the possibilities are endless!
- When memorising, always start with the VAI memory principle. It will help you make a better story and stronger connections if you are using *loci*.
- Be creative about ways to use memory techniques. You will be surprised at how many applications they have when you start experimenting.

Speed Reading Techniques

'Don't think, feel ... it is like a finger pointing a way to the moon. Don't concentrate on the finger or you will miss all that heavenly glory!'

— BRUCE LEE, *ENTER THE DRAGON*

I WAS NEVER A BIG READER. I didn't read many books in school. Even at university I struggled to read textbooks that were part of the required reading. Discovering speed reading was the most rewarding learning experience for me. It allowed me not only to start reading again, but also to enjoy it. I ended up reading all the books on my bookshelf once I got to grips with the techniques. Mind you, I only had a couple of books! But still, it was a huge accomplishment for me. So why is speed reading in a book on memory? The fact is that speed reading uses the same key principles, the same Yellow Elephant model. When speed reading, we move from step 1 — abstract to step 2 — image. The only difference is that the story (association) is already presented to you.

Use the following passage to test your current reading speed. Using a timer, record how long it takes you to read this passage as you normally would. Start your timer now!

Best Day Thinking

MARK DOBSON

Every skill has a corresponding feeling: when you are experiencing that exact feeling, the skill becomes a natural expression, needing little or no deliberate thought. For instance, when we laugh, the feeling naturally creates movement of the body. There are different theories about how feelings arise, but I lean towards the model that says feelings come from three ingredients: what you do with your body, what you do with your words and what you focus on. You don't see miserable people skipping down the street, because the body movement doesn't match the feeling. If you are miserable, try skipping for a few minutes and note how it changes you. Likewise, people in love don't just whisper about their feelings to their friends — instead, you see them happy to shout their love to the world, just as Tom Cruise did on Oprah's couch. Furthermore, if I wanted you to get angry, just telling you to get angry would not work, but changing your focus would. If I told you that your child's teacher hits and ridicules them in front of the class on a daily basis, that change of focus is enough to get you angry.

Of these ingredients — body, words, focus — I have found that focus is the one athletes need to address most. I have also found that when you get it right, it generates amazing power with very little effort.

To design the focus and thinking required for each athlete to perform at their best, I designed and use a model called 'Best Day thinking'. Essentially, it is about working out what an athlete focuses on when they have their *best* performance, then developing the ability to duplicate that thinking on days when they need their best performance. It works on the premise that there is a special mental recipe for experiencing the best days and performances, whereas on 'off' days you use a different recipe.

For example, there will be things that cause you to laugh spontaneously when you think about them. You just can't help it. Maybe it's remembering a time when a family member walked into a glass door they thought was open, or recalling a dinner party when your favourite uncle laughed so hard he launched his dentures onto the table. Now if we want you to go into a social environment and light up the room when you walk in, we simply need to have you talk about and focus on those funny occasions for the short time before you enter. You then can't help but have the feeling required to bring out your best social self. You instinctively walk in with a legitimate smile on your face. Compare that to times when you don't want to go to a function and, on the way, you have been talking about all the people you hope you don't get stuck talking to. You then walk in with a very contrived smile that people know is not real and you easily get tired from faking it. Your focus has had you under perform and use more energy.

Similarly, when an athlete is at their best they have things that they focus on that bring out the best of their ability and more. Just like a funny thought will move their body involuntarily, athletes have thoughts that help them excel involuntarily.

To find these, I simply ask the athlete to talk me through their favourite performance — or their imagined favourite performance, if they haven't had one yet. I get them to walk me through the day of their favourite performance and explain what their attitudes were about everything. Typically, you will find that their routine was much the same as on other days, but their attitudes and approaches were different. On a bad day, during their warm-up for the event, they might be focusing on how sore they are, while on their best day they feel just as sore but they know they are just warming up. On a bad day they might focus on how good all the other competitors look, while on their best day they laugh with their friends and don't even notice the other competitors.

It's pretty simple stuff, but it is crucial to be aware of and sensitive to these thoughts, because they are a recipe and if you change one ingredient in a recipe you get a different result. For instance, what happens if your athlete turns up to their event and they are laughing and chatting with friends? This may be their Best Day Thinking, which will bring out the best of their ability. But maybe you don't feel they are focused enough, so you call them over and have them look at all their competitors to think through a strategy. Logically, it sounds like a good idea, but if it's not in line with their Best Day Thinking you may have just dissolved their killer instinct by asking them to do it your way.

Some people will want to watch their competitors, and some will want to get fired up. Everyone is different, but if you want to bring out the best ability in someone, you need to find out what their Best Day Thinking is and allow it.

This is where positive thinking lacks some impact, because positive thinking often only needs to be used consciously on a bad day. For instance, the athlete's legs feel heavy today and we say to them, 'No, you'll be right, give them a shake. You can do it. You'll be OK when you get out there'. This sounds good, but to measure the effectiveness of this approach you need to compare it to how the athlete handles the same feelings of heavy legs on their 'best day'. If you already know what their Best Day Thinking is, you can remind them of it and they might respond by saying, 'My legs will be alright five minutes into the race'. This is a more powerful approach, as it recreates the recipe of their best performance.

If you do try to have a conversation with your athlete about their Best Day Thinking, you will often find they answer with, 'But when I am playing really well, I am not thinking about anything!' That is true. Often when we are at our best we are in a state of instinct, fully immersed in the task at hand. So ask them what their thinking is leading up to the competition. Ask: 'When you are heading to the game and you know you are going to nail it that day, what are you most excited about? What are you looking forward to?' or 'On your best day, when you feel tired but you still know you are going to have a great day, what is your attitude to your fatigue?' By asking questions such as these you will flush out what their focus is on their best days.

Now, as a coach, when I know an athlete's Best Day Thinking pattern, I never make them perform it like clockwork. When they are actually in the zone it is raw instinct; there is nothing contrived about their thought process at all. This means that Best Day Thoughts are actually the thoughts just before they enter the zone, not while they are in it. So when coaching at training or in competitions I just let the athlete enjoy their sport. It's only when I see them focusing on the wrong thing or getting distracted from their best recipe that I refocus them on their Best Day Thinking. Most of the time they don't even know I have done it. We just have a chat and they don't know why but they feel better.

There are times when an athlete gets so lost that they cannot get out of their negativity or 'Worst Day' recipe. I try to catch them early before their negative mindset becomes too entrenched and they can't shake it off, but this is not always possible. If your athlete gets really negative, Best Day Thinking won't work until you first break their negative mood. To do this, you need to catch them off guard. Challenge them to a farting contest, loudest fart wins. Pour your drink over their head. Lie down in the street. Do anything that creates any emotion in them which is different to their negative one. Once they snap out of that mood, remind them of a Best Day Thought.

This tool, Best Day Thinking, can refocus an athlete if they have become too mechanical and lost their killer instinct. It can also set them up to be in their zone for competition. Most of all, just by letting an athlete know that they can have a different mental focus in competition and in practice will help them reconnect with their innate instinct.

1475 words

Stop your timer!

To calculate your reading speed, divide the number of words in the text (1475) by the number of minutes it took you to read. For example, if you read the piece in 6:30:

$$1475 \div 6.5 = 227 \text{ words per minute (wpm)}$$

The average adult reading speed is about 240 wpm, with about 63 per cent comprehension. This might seem quite high, but in reality we can read ten to twenty times faster with the right speed reading techniques. People who read a lot tend to be more in the 300 to 400 wpm range. Not many people in the world can read more than 400 wpm. The speed reading techniques in this book can get you to read over 1500 wpm with better comprehension.

What is Speed Reading?

Due to its name, most people think speed reading is just reading really fast. Some people say that speed reading is reading so fast that you miss out or 'skim' words, only focusing on certain key

words. This is actually a myth. Speed reading is a strategy to not only read faster, but also to have far greater comprehension. Many people then ask: 'How is this possible? How can you understand more by reading faster? It doesn't make sense!'

Let's think about what happens when we're driving.

Imagine you are driving your car on the highway. The sign says 100 kilometres per hour (km/h), but you are only doing 10 km/h. Describe how you feel.

_____

_____

Now picture yourself driving in a residential area. This time you are driving at 160 km/h in a 60-kilometre zone. Describe how you feel below.

_____

_____

For driving very slowly in a 100-kilometre zone, you might have written:
- slow
- bored
- taking longer to reach the destination
- frustrated
- not concentrating
- less focused
- more thoughts inside my head
- distracted

For driving extremely fast in a residential area, you might have written:

- dangerous
- fast
- exhilarated
- concentrating hard
- more focused
- no time to think of anything else besides drive and steer the best I can
- scared
- reaching destination in record time

Now let's think about this in terms of speed reading. If we read slowly, which is the case for most of us, it can feel very tedious. We become bored and take a long time to finish what we are reading. We become frustrated as we have to keep going back to revisit a word or a paragraph because it didn't quite stick in our heads — we were thinking of what we were going to have for dinner that night or what we were going to wear on the weekend instead.

If we suddenly tried to read faster, yes, we might find it 'dangerous' in that we would end up skipping words and our comprehension would thus suffer. However, using speed reading techniques to read faster results in greater comprehension and focus, allowing you to remember more of what you read. Because you will be reading fast, there is no time for distractions — you are focused on speed and strategy. Before you know it, you will have finished reading and have a much better understanding of the content!

The strategies that will help you achieve this are:

- conscious competence
- using a reading guide

- chunking
- image flow

Conscious Competence

Sometimes people read a word or sentence two or more times because they realise they have missed something. This is called rereading. It happens because our brain hasn't registered the images from those words (the shift from abstract to image has not happened), and thus the brain is still trying to catch up while we are already reading further ahead. As a result, we have to reread so we can capture the visual for that piece of information. As people often read word by word, the brain gets tired after a while from processing all those words, so more rereading occurs.

Imagine you are sitting down to watch a movie at home and one of your family members or friends rewinds for 10 seconds because they missed a part. Then they rewind another 10 seconds in a moment's time. Then another. Right throughout the whole movie. How would that feel? The two-hour movie may now go for six hours because of the constant rewinding. Your brain will be tired and it will break your concentration on and involvement with the movie as well. This is exactly what happens when you reread. You are constantly interrupted, and the reading material takes much longer than it should. I never read many books when I was younger because I found myself rereading many times over and still not understanding.

We want to be able to read smoothly and without interruptions. Hence, not going back to reread is a vital element in speed reading. I know you're probably asking: 'If you don't go back, don't you miss the important words or actually misunderstand what you've read?' The answer is no, not if you learn to effectively use the speed reading techniques, which assist your comprehension overall.

So how do we do this?

First, let's see how often you currently reread. Read the section below *as you would naturally* and keep a tally of every occasion when you find yourself rereading a word or phrase. By the end of the section total up the number of times you reread.

An Introduction to Naturopathy

JULIDE TURKER

Naturopathy is a holistic system of healing that incorporates a range of treatments and natural therapies, with the underlying belief that your body is able to fight infection and disease itself, given the right support. While conventional medicine is preoccupied with treating the symptoms of a disease or illness, naturopathy takes a more holistic approach to healthcare, with a patient's overall health a priority. Naturopaths are typically accredited by national associations, which ensure that they have undergone the required training and comply with the highest standards of naturopathic practice.

Naturopaths believe that if one restores or maintains the equilibrium of the body, our immune system is better placed to defend itself against infection and disease. There is therefore no use of or reliance on medication as such — this would only serve to suppress the symptoms of an illness. A naturopath is more likely to recommend a program of exercise, a change in diet or a natural treatment than prescribe any drugs. Natural treatments and therapies are used to ensure that the body and mind are able to remain resilient and recover promptly. When we do succumb to an illness and, for example, contract a fever, this is viewed as the body dealing with the source of the problem. The fever is therefore not viewed as a negative event, rather as part of the body's natural defence system.

Illness is a purposeful process of the organism. The process of healing includes the generation of symptoms that are, in fact, an expression of the life force attempting to heal itself. Therapeutic actions should be complementary to and synergistic with this healing process. The physician's actions can support or antagonise the actions of the *vis mediatrix nature* — the healing power of nature. Therefore, methods designed to suppress symptoms without removing the underlying causes are considered harmful and to be avoided or minimised.

The body has an inherent ability to establish, maintain and restore health. The healing process is ordered and intelligent; nature heals through the response of the life force. The physician's role is to facilitate this process, to identify and remove obstacles to health and recovery, and to establish or restore a healthy internal and external environment.

Underlying causes of disease must be discovered and removed or treated before a person can recover completely from illness. Symptoms express the body's attempt to heal, but are not the cause or disease. Symptoms, therefore, should not be suppressed by treatment. Causes may occur on many levels, including physical, mental, emotional and spiritual. The physician must evaluate fundamental underlying causes on all levels, directing treatment at root causes rather than at symptomatic expression.

Health and disease are conditions of the whole organism, a whole involving the complex interaction of many factors. The naturopathic physician must treat the whole person by taking these factors into account. The harmonious functioning of physical, mental, emotional and spiritual aspects are essential to recovery from and prevention of disease. This requires a comprehensive approach to diagnosis and treatment.

The Physician as Teacher

A cooperative doctor-patient relationship has inherent therapeutic value. The physician's major role is to educate and encourage the patient to take responsibility for their own health. The physician is a catalyst for healthful change, empowering and motivating the patient to assume responsibility. It is the patient, not the doctor, who ultimately creates/accomplishes healing. Teaching with hope, knowledge and understanding, the physician acts to enable patients to heal.

The ultimate goal of any healthcare system should be prevention of disease. This is accomplished through education and promotion of life habits that create good health. The physician learns to assess risk factors and to sharpen their deductive reasoning and understand the patient's circumstances. Appropriate interventions are then sought to avoid further harm or risk to the patient. Building health works better and more surely than fighting disease.

Who can Benefit from Naturopathy?

Quite possibly you! Health is not the absence of a diagnosed disease; health is the ability to wake up in the morning looking forward to your day, when your physical, emotional and mental well-being are experiencing synergy and are in harmony.

You can see a naturopath for anything you would consult your GP for: weight loss/gain, fatigue, hormonal conditions, fatty liver disease, auto-immune issues, high blood pressure, cholesterol, type I and type II diabetes and anything else that is primarily due to a nutritional and/or energetic imbalance.

730 words

So how many times did you reread? Very few people read without going back on a word here and there; most of us go back at least three or four times in a passage of this length. Although this might not sound like many times. Over a number of pages it adds up, just like in our movie rewind example.

Now read the passage again, but this time make a conscious effort *not to go back and reread.* Try and resist any urge to go back, and force yourself to move forward. Once again, tally the number of times you reread.

We call this conscious competence because it involves making a mindful effort about the activity you are undertaking (reading). The competence in this case refers to 'competently' moving forward without going back to reread. If you were unable to do this, then you would be at the stage of conscious incompetence, whereby you are mindful of moving forward but just unable to execute going forward without rereading quite yet. Your aim is to practice until you achieve conscious competence, whereby you have completely eliminated rereading.

Rereading Action Plan

Use the following table to record your rereading action plan. For each session, select a few pages from any reading material (book, magazine, internet) and tally up the number of times you reread. You can also time yourself and record your speed (using the method shown on page 55), so that you can see how you improve over time.

Date	Reading material	Numbers of times rereading occurred	Speed

Using a Reading Guide

When I was at school, people who used their finger to follow what they were reading were considered 'dumb'. Unfortunately, this belief still exists today. In fact, reading with your finger is one of the best things to do for your reading as it helps you to concentrate on what you're reading: it's one way of using a reading guide.

A reading guide is a pointing device used for following words when reading. When we read, normally our eyes have no guide, meaning they drift, and rereading occurs. By using a reading guide you can get your eyes to perfectly follow your reading without any rereading. Your reading guide can be your finger, a pen, a business card … whatever is easy for you.

To use a reading guide effectively, place it underneath the first word and move it across to the following words as you read. Remember the first technique? While you are doing this, also make a conscious effort not to reread. You will soon find that with a bit of practice you are reading with greater speed, and you will develop your own way of comfortably using the reading guide. The use of the guide will further assist you to avoid rereading and you will tend to find that your guide will move faster than your eyes: this will cause you to play 'catch up' with your guide, making you read faster.

Practise using a reading guide on the text below:

The Desert Rats

TRISTAN MILLER

I don't remember why I went to the desert. I know I'd made the decision to go long before I had even looked at the website. I'd been speaking with a buddy about what our next marathon should be and he started rambling on about all the great races around the world we could be doing.

'If only we had a shit ton of cash and endless holidays,' said Scotty. He'd been reading his *10 Epic Races to Do before you Die* book again. 'We could do the Western States 100 mile, or the Marathon des Sables. It's 250 km across the Sahara! How rad would that be?'

I listened and visualised the pages in his book. They showed a column of runners, caked in pale yellow dust, inching across the dramatic sand dunes of the fabled Sahara. Nobody was running. They were just drifting with the sand. My mouth became parched as I wondered how I would cope in that kind of challenge.

I snapped out of my daydream and Scott was still babbling about some race in Alaska. I agreed, but swung the conversation back to reality. We settled on a more domestic destination, the Gold Coast Marathon, and went back to the daily grind of training and work.

I loved having the challenge of a marathon to tick off once or twice a year. It made me feel invincible to have the kind of fitness that comes with pushing myself through 42 km, revelling in the glory of completing my task. It helped me focus at work, stay motivated when things got rough, plus look super fit as I eased into my thirties!

But marathons are a set distance, so after the first few races, where you experience huge improvements in time, the most you can hope for is to shave off a few minutes with a solid performance or have a stab at the ethereal sub-three hours.

An ultra marathon is considered to be anything beyond 42.2 km. Which essentially means from 43 km to infinity! There is no cap, making it a frightening concept. Most ultra runners don't consider anything under 50 km will fit the bill, so they look for 100 km or 160 km races to test their mettle. I had become enamoured with the idea that I could run further than a marathon, even touch up to 90-100 km. It was a secret desire, but one which grew with my confidence as a runner.

In 2009, I lost my plum job at Google during the Global Financial Crisis. They shut my office and I was disturbed about it. Luckily I had already committed to the most famous road ultra in the world — the Comrades ultra marathon in South Africa, 89 km from Pietermaritzburg to Durban. It was tough, but I was tougher. It inspired me to think differently. I came up with a radical plan to outrun the Global Crisis … or at least kill some time 'til things settled down.

I was going to step way outside my comfort zone by running 52 marathons in the 52 weeks of 2010. I'd throw a couple of 100 km races in there, to see if I could break myself. And I'd run in a different country each week, so by the end of that year, I'd covered races in 42 countries and on all 7 continents — including Antarctica! I know … epic!

But after that crazy year, I knew I'd need an even bigger goal to work towards, or I'd have a massive come down to deal with. So while I was still travelling in 2010, I booked myself a spot in the Marathon des Sables, for 2 April 2011. I talked Scotty into it too. It didn't take much, as there was no way he could miss out on that adventure.

I trained as much as I could from January to April in 2011. But the fact is I was pretty broken from 2010. Plus, there are no deserts for at least 1000 km in any direction from Melbourne, Australia, so where do you practise for an environment like the Sahara?

So when Scott and I flew into Morocco, I was a little anxious. When we crossed the Atlas Mountains to Ouarzazate, on the edge of the Sahara, I became obviously concerned. Then we headed to the start line bivouac in army trucks and I knew I was in trouble. It was hot and gritty. Hell, it was a desert. Everyone was sweating buckets and messing around with their kit, comparing items with the 900 other cowboys who'd decided running 250 km across a desert was a good idea.

There are a number of factors that add to the difficulty of this race:

- It gets over 50°C in the daytime and they start the race at 9 am, so you can soak it up.

- You have to carry freeze-dried food for the seven days, plus sleeping kit and fresh undies if you are so inclined.

- You must have 1.5 l of water at the beginning of each day. You are rationed three to six bottles of water throughout each day. Depending on distance.

- You run 250 km over six days, sleeping in open tents each night.

- It is devastatingly hot in the day (+50°C) and bloody freezing cold in the night (5°C or below).

- Small grains of sand rub large holes in your skin — be it toes or crotch — all day, every day.

- Each day is a different distance — the longest is 82 km and the shortest just 16 km.

- The terrain is extremely varied — hills, dunes, canyons and river beds — with each new space feeling like a new type of torture.

- Frequent sand storms can hinder your vision and have you eating a kilo of sand each day.

We finally got moving on day one, with ACDC's 'Highway to Hell' blaring across the start line. Most people were as anxious as I was, but they sang along anyway, full of false bravado. A few were old hands in this race. Moroccans usually stood on the podium and Euro challengers made a play for the rest of the top ten. They seemed very tuned in to the race conditions, while I was more concerned that my number was in its correct position.

That first day wasn't too bad. The small section of dunes was a shock, but it was achievable. We trotted across the finish line and Scotty and I immediately compared notes. Apart from the lack of vision during a short sand storm, we figured we could get through this ordeal in one piece.

That night, however, one of the other Australians, Paul, started to vomit. By morning he was shivering and the every-present medical team had him on an intravenous drip, while covering him in blankets, to slow his descent into a dangerous state of hypothermia. We looked on with naked fear. It showed us not to become complacent: nobody was safe.

At 6 am, the 'Blue Fury' would swarm our bivouac and take down the tents around us. This was a large team of young Moroccans in blue smocks who packed up the whole encampment, loaded it onto old army trucks and dragged it across this wasteland to the day's next destination. Each day it felt like they had come five minutes earlier, just to catch us sleeping.

We'd eat, pack our gear, fill our bottles with water and make our way to the start line as the heat of the day crept across the desert. Then ACDC. Then run. Then hurt. Then push and pull ourselves over each hill and across each stretch of dust. Many hours later, the finish line would loom and a cup of Moroccan tea was your only stage reward. That and rest.

Runners pulled out every day for one reason or another. One German snapped his leg in the sand dunes — his body continued forward, while his foot remained caught in the deep sand. A French man had a heart attack and was airlifted to Paris. We found out the following day that he was still alive.

Each day, we'd wait to see if our friends made it. Those people in your tent were your closest companions. They were who you worried about the most. As they'd arrive, we'd check them off and see how much damage they had received in the day's battle with the desert. Could they go on? Could I go on?

Then food. A few jokes. Flaps of skin removed. Cuts covered in antiseptic. Sleep. Nightmares. The Blue Fury returns … repeat.

Another day closer. A few more kilometres each day. I knew I'd get there. Scott seemed impervious to the pain, but I knew he was just hiding it well. I'm glad he was there. He let me complain until I started to joke again.

We kept running, grinding, walking. I watched as people dropped in the sand ahead of me. One Spanish guy just sat with his head in his hands by the path. I tried to encourage him, but he waved me away. Another fella laughed maniacally as he took off his shoes halfway through a stage and walked on blistered feet, unable to endure the confines of his boots. We tried to talk him out of it, but madness was clear in his eyes and he kept moving forward on what would become a bloodied mess.

At one point, in the 82 km stage, I found myself alone in the desert. I couldn't see anyone ahead, nor anyone behind. I was afraid at first. Then nearly happy ... happy isn't right, but I was too close to crazy to call it anything else. I was just looking about, feeling like another grain of sand, blowing across this broad, wild space they call the Sahara.

Scott and I prevailed, along with 70 per cent of starters from so many nations. We kept moving till it was over and cried a little at the end. Not many tears would come, as we had no fluid left. We were hollow, spent, near broken men.

I couldn't talk about it much in the weeks that followed. I was traumatised by the whole ordeal. One evening, months later, I opened up about the adventure to my wife. I tried to explain it and made jokes about it. I tried to reconcile in my mind why I had gone to the desert. It still didn't make much sense and I don't know if I'll ever put it right in my head.

I don't know why I need to see what's out there. I know I'm a richer man for the experiences. Perhaps the Sahara was a step too far. Maybe it was one more step in the right direction of my life ...

1801 words

How did you go using a reading guide? The first thing you may notice is that your speed increased. It is possible to double your reading speed just by using a reading guide really well.

Reading Guide Action Plan

Using a reading guide, practise reading without rereading. Use the following table to record your action plan.

Date	Reading Material	Numbers of times rereading occurred	Speed

Speed Reading Tips

- Aim to improve your reading times if you are timing yourself. Reducing rereading is the key to speed reading. Once you have mastered these techniques, further techniques will be even easier. Aim to eliminate rereading altogether! This will provide a good base for you moving on to further speed reading techniques.

- If you are not comfortable with your reading guide, try an alternative guide such as a block of post-it notes or a business card. The most important factor in speed reading is that you are comfortable. If you're noticing that you're seeing the upcoming words as you read, try moving the guide beneath the words a bit further and faster. This will assist with keeping your brain aligned with the text you're reading.

- If you're not understanding what you're reading, try the opposite and read a tad slower using the technique. Do not rush! You will notice that rereading will be minimised, if not totally eliminated. As you continue practising you will naturally start to read faster without going back.

- It can also be helpful to underline keywords as you read. This will help you not to return back to words you believe you need to reread. It will also help you connect with what you're reading.

Chunking Technique for Speed Reading

When I was young, I was told to read word by word very carefully. While this was useful for the early stages of learning, it is counterproductive later in life. The ultimate purpose of speed reading isn't actually to read fast: it is to form images of what you read. In essence, it is really reading in images.

Let's take a sentence:

**The big fat cat jumped over
the large spiky fence.**

Reading this word by word, our brain processes ten words. Hypothetically, if every word took us one second to read, the above sentence would take ten seconds to read.

Now let's break the sentence into chunks.

**(The big fat cat) (jumped over)
(the large spiky fence)**

In this instance, we have 'chunked' the words into three (bracketed) images. If it took you one second to read each 'chunk' or image, the sentence could now be read in three seconds. This is more than three times faster than reading word by word! And you still read every word.

In order to apply chunking, we apply it to a minimum set of words. To begin with, start by taking three words at a time.

How to chunk:

1. Place your reading guide in the middle of the three words (i.e. beneath the second word).

2. Instead of reading each word, look at them as a group and visualise an image for them.

Practise chunking three words at a time when reading the text below.

Personal Brand: Your Professional Presence and Impact

JAMES FREEMANTLE

'Why should I work on my personal brand?' This is the question people most often ask about the work we do at my company, REDgum Communications. My answer is always the same, and it's a question: 'Do you want to influence people more effectively, so that they're more likely to take the actions you want them to take?' If the answer is 'yes', then you need to work on your professional presence and impact — your personal brand. And for those who say 'I don't want to have a personal brand', it's too late! Everyone has one. It's up to you to determine what you want it to be, so that you achieve your goals quickly and effectively, surrounded by positivity and clarity.

Personal brand simply means 'the way you are experienced by others'. To put it another way, if, after you interact with anyone, they talk about you, that description is your personal brand for that person in that situation. The accumulation of such descriptions over time shapes your brand. Brand — as marketers know — is a promise of a consistent experience to a consumer. So the more people experience you and talk about you in consistent and positive ways, the stronger and more effective your personal brand.

In my job, I help people examine the visual, vocal and verbal elements of interpersonal interaction as well as the behaviours they display in pressure situations. We help identify clients' optimal professional presence and impact — based on their values, goals, strengths and needs — and hone the skills required to achieve this presence.

The first time I had to stand up in front of a casting agent and perform an audition, I was struck dumb by stage fright. I forgot my lines, my mouth went dry and my hands shook. I lost my ability to communicate my optimal personal brand effectively with my audience. Needless to say, I missed out on the role!

Before long, though, I was working in front of a TV camera every week, being asked to speak to large groups about personal brand, media and presentation skills, and training corporate and education professionals in Singapore, Vietnam and throughout Australia.

One job was with the Law Faculty at the University of Melbourne, teaching jurists from Vietnam, Indonesia and Mongolia to communicate and present effectively in their workplaces. For lawyers and judges, the workplace is often a courtroom, where they need to address juries, cross-examine witnesses, negotiate, deliver rulings and practise advocacy. They need, in essence, to have performance skills. And yet the focus of these people was frequently on their content only. The method I prefer uses skills from theatre, exhorts the need to identify ways in which people are currently being — and want to be — experienced, and identifies action and feeling goals to achieve the required audience impact. For example, you might want every person in your audience to subscribe to your newsletter, so to maximise the chance of them taking that action, you will need to make them feel something that causes them to take that action. This feeling might be 'inspired', 'greedy' or even 'FoMO' (fearful of missing out)! But whatever the feeling you set as your goal, it's up to you to make sure your client feels it. Maya Angelou put it best when she said, 'I've learnt that people will forget what you said, people will forget what you did, but people will never forget the way you made them feel.'

Let's take a look at athletes for some tips on the successful and not-so-successful creation of personal brand. Most

Olympians go to the Olympic Games to take part. Only a small number win a medal. Most simply aim to do their best — achieve a personal best. A personal best says that I have acquitted myself to the peak of my ability, fulfilled my potential at this point in time. Most personal bests go largely unnoticed unless they come with a medal or a WWPB (world's worst personal best)! A WWPB entails finishing excessively far behind the other competitors. Equatorial Guinean 'Eric the Eel' — the dog-paddler from the Sydney 2000 Olympic Games — and eccentric aerialist 'Eddie the Eagle', who represented Great Britain in the Calgary Winter Olympic Games in 1988, are good examples of personal bests that were pretty bad but represented the spirit of the Games. From the Jamaican bobsled team and Australian Steven Bradbury, the speed skater who stayed standing when others fell to take gold, to the likes of Michael Phelps and Usain Bolt, the best and the 'worst' etch their stories into the collective consciousness.

Being in the spotlight of the world brings opportunity for athletes, and personal brands are both built and destroyed under such microscopic coverage. How athletes conduct themselves during and after their events defines how we perceive them. Think drugs-tainted Canadian sprinter Ben Johnson or, from the London Olympic Games, our ringleted ex-golden-boy Steve Hooker. He was supposed to bring home gold for us, but he didn't clear a height in the pole vault final. And 'The Missile', James Magnussen, didn't do as well as we wanted or felt we deserved. But boy he grew up! He'll be great in Rio in 2016. It's the way we experience these icons through the lens of the media that determines how we feel about them — and that's what makes a brand.

Usain Bolt blows away all comers on the track, then puts on a show and talks to everyone. We love him, and — kerching! — don't his sponsors too! At the other end of the speed scale, rower Hamadou Djibo Issaka came last by a long way in the 2000 metre single sculls at the 2012 Olympic Games, but the crowd loved him and he has inspired others in Niger to take up rowing. Inspiring others might well lead him into a lucrative speaking career or into coaching. Like Seb Coe, he might have a stellar career in administration. Whether athletes excel or just try hard, if they are good sports and they're personable, we like them and we aspire to be like them. And that makes them personal brand gold medallists.

'Does social media play a role?' people ask. It most certainly does! The likes of Twitter and Facebook invite us into the lives of our young champions. They let us get to know, almost as we would friends, those stars we 'follow'. When Lauren Jackson tweeted 'PEACE AND LOVE precious people. Kisses', her 72,700 followers went to sleep smiling. In contrast, many frowned on Nick D'Arcy and Kenrick Monk posing with guns in a photo published on Facebook. In a corporate context, a social media tidal wave can engulf or propel a company, with huge ramifications. Coca-Cola is under siege in an ongoing campaign to make it more environmentally and socially accountable. BP was lambasted as a result of the Gulf of Mexico oil spill and its CEO's apparent lack of genuine concern about the incident.

But back to Olympians: if one personal brand has been a roller-coaster it's that of Oscar Pistorius. When teammate Ofentse Mogawane crashed to the track in the semifinal of the 4 × 400 metres relay, the 'Blade Runner' entered a world of pain. In his body language, there was no apparent concern for his comrade writhing in pain on the track. Oscar held his head in his hands as he saw the chance to compete in a final in open competition slip away. This was an insight into the man's character which didn't enhance his brand. Compare this to John Landy stopping to help the fallen Ron Clarke in the 1500 metre national final in 1956 — still one of the worlds's most often cited acts of sportsmanship. Landy went on to win the race, and in an ironic twist Pistorius too went on to get his run in the final, on appeal. But in one way, he'd missed a chance. Furthermore, his brand has subsequently been under extraordinary scrutiny and in great jeopardy since he allegedly shot and killed his girlfriend Reeva Steenkamp on Valentine's Day the following year.

Some think personal brands only apply to celebrities, but like it or not we all have a brand: the experiences others have of us. And just like an Olympic athlete, you can get the training, coaching and mentoring you need to improve your personal best, your personal brand.

So what's mine? Well here's the official version: Based in Moscow during 2007-08, James Freemantle was an international anchor for twenty-four-hour TV news channel *Russia Today*, broadcasting to Europe, the United States and the United Kingdom. James is well known for his experiential travel stories on Australian television between 1998 and 2007. He's written, produced and presented over 300 stories for Australian television — on the Seven Network's *Coxy's Big Break*, the Nine Network's *Postcards* and *Talk to the Animals*, and Network Ten's *Bread*. James has degrees in English, history and education, is accredited is DiSC behavioural analysis, and has travelled extensively. James is a mental health advocate for SANE Australia, and through REDgum is charity partner of the Entrust Foundation — wise philanthropy in the developing world — and Ladder — tackling youth homelessness.

I'm also a father, a husband, and a lover of fitness, reading, trees and the sea. In every business interaction I have, I've settled on the following three words as those I'd most like people to use to describe me, and they best sum up my personal brand: Strong. Positive. Clear.

What are your three words?

1593 Words

Chunking Action Plan

Use your own materials to practise the art of chunking. Fill in the date and list the type of material you're reading (for example newspaper, textbook, comic) and then write down the size of chunk you used while reading. Over time, you will be able to increase your chunk size, but more importantly you will notice an increase in reading comprehension.

Date	Reading material	Chunk size	Speed

You should aim to build up to chunking at least five words together at a time. If you are timing yourself, also aim to improve your speed. You can challenge yourself by reading at double your chunk size!

If you are having difficulty chunking, try reading a tad slower using the techniques. Do not rush! You will notice that rereading will slowly reduce, if not be totally eliminated. As you continue your practice you will naturally start to read faster without going back.

Image Flow Technique for Speed Reading

While chunking works well, it may not provide you with the best images, as you may have to chunk a group of words that doesn't necessarily make sense as an image, such as 'this and …' Image flow is a technique that assists you to visualise and capture images from the words that are shown. If we take our previous chunking example:

(The big fat cat) (jumped over the)
(large spiky fence)

With image flow, we can see that it might make more sense to have:

(The big fat cat jumped over)
(the large spiky fence)

or

(The big fat cat jumped over the
large spiky fence)

In the first case, the big fat cat jumping forms one image and the spiky large fence forms another: two in total. In the second, we're able to picture both the cat and the fence in the one image.

The trick is to identify the images as you read. Once you get the hang of this technique, it will really boost your speed and comprehension, as you are now capturing more information with fewer images.

Practise your image flow for the reading below.

Financial Crisis or Families in Crisis?

MONIQUE TOOHEY

The financial crisis affects no other institution as much as it does families dependent on employment and a secure income. When that employment or source of financial security suddenly disappears, it can leave many families under huge pressure as they fight to pay mortgages or rent, food, petrol, medicine and school fees: the never-ending list of debits from their bank accounts goes on and on.

Financial stress also places another type of account under pressure: the emotional bank account. This account is invisibly held between spouses or between parents and children. When there is nothing left in one of these emotional bank accounts, credit turns to debt and relationships suffer and can and often do ultimately break down.

So what is an emotional bank account?

An emotional bank account is sort of like the 'brownie points' we are awarded when we do something nice for another person. For example, a husband buys his wife flowers and in doing so he notches up a few brownie or bonus points that unconsciously go into the 'I feel good about you' account. A four-week-old infant smiles at her parents for the first time: that's massive in the points department, particularly after many sleepless nights! When I refer to brownie points, I am talking about positive emotion or feeling good, happy, sometimes even over the moon about a person you have a relationship with. When another person does something nice for us, we generally feel good about them and the relationship we have with them. As a result of this exchange and feel-good activity, the relationship can improve. Even when your local baker throws in two bread rolls for free, we feel really good about them. These exchanges of goodness assist relationship building and relationship maintenance.

Of course, the opposite is also true. When spouses stop doing those little things for each other, like making each other cups of tea, helping each other to achieve goals or perhaps just sending an SMS to the other person while at work to quickly say 'I love you', the relationship's resilience in times of stress, such as after a disagreement or when experiencing financial difficulties, diminishes. When we feel really good about our partner or child, we make more excuses for those little annoyances, and indeed we have more patience for each other. If the emotional bank account is running very low — say less than a quarter full — the other three quarters fill up with animosity and resentment, and hurt lingers longer. If the relationship is running on a lot less than a quarter of a cup, usually the only things holding it together are children, familial or cultural expectations, dependency or financial obligations. It loses the status of a marriage/relationship and is downgraded to an 'arrangement'. We hold emotional bank accounts with everyone we have a relationship with: not just with our spouses and children, but also with our stepchildren and even our in-laws.

So here is a golden rule: if you contribute to your relationship with kindness, don't expect anything in return — it is simply a fabulous investment in your relationship. Kindness needs to flow both ways in order to maintain a healthy relationship.

Couples often ignore the emotional needs of one another out of mindlessness (not paying attention), not malice. It is important to communicate to each other about the types of kind deeds that will actually top up a bank account. Some often quoted by couples include respectful communication, physical affection (more often stated by men), paying attention and spending time doing fun activities, helping out around the house (more often stated by women), small gifts, flowers and eating together.

It is important not to track each other's contributions or turn it into a competition: 'I did this many things for you this week!' That won't be helpful. Even during hard times, it is important to continue to strive to do nice things for each other, especially those that cost nothing. Even a reassuring smile is a gift.

Families with good relationships not only do nice things for each other but they also notice up to 50 per cent more of the loving gestures of other family members towards them.

Finally, choose your emotional investment wisely. Get input from your spouse or children about the emotional areas that they believe need some of your loving attention and you'll make a memorable impact and perhaps yield a greater return.

738 words

Image flow is a more difficult technique, so keep persisting if it doesn't work straight away. Try visualising the images more slowly, taking your time to create mental pictures. As you get better, you can increase your speed.

Here are some tips to help you with image flow.

- Look at the group of words slowly and try and grasp the image from them.
- Once you get the hang of image flow, read faster.
- Make sure you get good solid practice on various types of reading material.
- Challenge yourself by seeing more images at one time.

OK, so now you have learnt all four speed reading techniques.

Test yourself on the reading passage below, using your favourite technique or a range of techniques. This reading passage is a bit more technical, so you can work harder at creating images. You can always go back to any of the previous reading passages to test out your new skills. The more practice you get, the quicker and better your reading will be!

Entrepreneurship

DR JANUSZ TANAS

An entrepreneur is a dynamic and visionary businessperson who bears the risks imposed by changes in market demand. An entrepreneur spurs and reshapes economic growth and serves as a catalyst in the development of transitional economies, filling niches, improving societal existence and, as a result, overall politico-economic progress.

Purpose

The major raison d'être of this paper is to illustrate the meaning of the French word *entrepreneur,* outlining the depth of its philosophical significance.

Hoselitz (1962) argues that the word *entrepreneur* originated in the twelfth century in Europe from the French word *entreprendre,* meaning 'to undertake'. Three hundred years later, the evolved verb and noun form of the term emerged and entered the English language (Formaini, 2001). In 1730, the French Physiocrat Richard Cantillion (Hebert and Link, 1982) in his work *Essai sur la Nature du Commerce en Général* first introduced the concept of the entrepreneur into economic analysis. He used *entrepreneur* to mean a self-employed person who accepted the risk that he believed was natural in providing for one's own economic prosperity. Cantillion ([1755] 1959) described the entrepreneur in the classic sense as a great business adventurer with vision, who bears the risks imposed by the changes in the market demand. Cantillion's (1964) view was derived from both his career as an economic theorist and from his position as one of the wealthiest men in Europe. He has been credited with being the first world economic theorist to develop a scientific economic methodology and to develop a systematic understanding of the economy (Formaini, 2001; Rothbard, 1995; Spengler, 1960; Thornton, 1998; Vérin, 1982).

Although Cantillion's (1730) *Essai sur la Nature du Commerce en Général* came first, the leader of this economic model was Francois Quesnay, a surgeon who turned to medicine as the result of weakening eyesight. Cantillion created the term *Physiocracy,* which in his view is fundamentally an economic theory that creates the wealth of nations exclusively from agriculture. Thus, in Cantillion's (1730) analysis, the land was the essential source of the creation of wealth. Physiocrats, distressed with the deteriorating economic affairs of France, undertook the drive to reform the process of wealth creation to benefit overall society. Physiocrats originally called themselves *les économistes,* as they were the first to develop the idea of being of 'economically' astute (Formaini, 2001; Hoselitz, 1962; Spengler, 1960).

The term *Physiocracy* is derived from the Greek *physis* (nature) and *kràtos* (power), meaning 'government of nature'. It was perhaps the first well-developed theory of economics, originating from the Greek *oikonomikos.* One may note that the term *economy* was originally introduced in Ancient Greek times as **οικονομία,** a contraction of the noun **oiko,** meaning 'house', 'room', 'family' and 'household', and the verb **viμειv,** meaning 'to organise, distribute, manage and use' — thus, 'skilled in household management' (Finley 1973, 1999). The foundation of entrepreneurial activities can be detected in works by the Greek philosophers (1) Hesoid (700 BCE), who stated that the household is to be regarded as an ethical obligation, and (2) Xenophon (394 BCE), who in his *Cyropaedia* unveiled principals regarding the division of work and use of specialization, whereas (3)

Aristotle (340 BCE) addressed rationality of planning and decision-making (Freiling, 2005; Karayiannis).

The Physiocrats believed in the concept of *laissez faire, laissez passer* — 'let them do it' — meaning that they believed in a natural order of things, not to be selfish but to respect the common well-being of society. Furthermore, their vision was to create a reliable legal order for all groups of society to allow maximum freedom for people to start and operate businesses, consequently creating the coherence and well-being of the entire population (Formaini, 2001; Hoselitz, 1962).

A comparable view is presented by Francois Quesnay in *Tableau Économique* (1759), which first appeared in the Marquis de Mirabeau's *L'ami des Hommes* (1760). His judgement about entrepreneurs resembled Cantillion's, when he referred to the land-owning entrepreneurs who guide food production through uncertainty, organize and supervise production, introduce new methods and new products, and explore new markets (Hoselitz, 1962). Most authors believed that the entrepreneur must rely on the government to provide freedom of decision-making to undertake the venture (Formaini, 2001).

Other French economists, including Abbé Nicolas Baudeau and Anne-Rober-Jacques Turgot (Baron de l'Aulne), supported Cantillion's views that the entrepreneur is an intelligent, wealthy and adventurous individual (Hébert and Link, 1982). Baudeau ([1771] 1910), suggested the function of the entrepreneur was to be an innovator, thereby bringing invention and innovation into the discussion. According to philosopher and political economist Jacques Turgot (1977), the entrepreneur should hold larger profits than the landlord in order to subsidise his risks and work.

In the light of very basic and limited financial markets and with institutionally supplied capital being uncommon, Cantillion viewed the entrepreneur as simply a risk taker under conditions of uncertainty, who used his own capital to support entrepreneurial activities. He argued that the risk involved was not only financial but also one associated with the opportunity costs of time and expertise (Kanbur, 1980). However, French political economist researchers developed the relationship between entrepreneurs and the source of capital for economic innovation. In other words, they contributed to be the development of external financial markets (Formaini, 2001; Hoselitz, 1962).

With the commencement of the Industrial Revolution (1830), Jean-Baptise Say (1803), a French textile manufacturer and economist made the term popular in his *Traité d'Economie Politique*. Say expanded the definition of a successful entrepreneur to include the possession of managerial skills as an important element of entrepreneurship. He wrote that the entrepreneur needed a combination of moral qualities, such as judgement, perseverance and knowledge of the world, as well as the skills of operating a business. Entrepreneurs must be able to predict, forecast, evaluate and undertake risk. Bearing the risk meant making decisions under conditions of uncertainty, which was the entrepreneurs' raison d'être. Moreover, he claimed that entrepreneurs had to be leaders who lead and manage other people in order to achieve their goals (Barreto, 1989; Formaini, 2001; Long, 1983; Rothbard, 1995; Schumpeter, 1951; Scott, 1933; Spengler, 1960).

Jean-Baptiste Say (1803) strongly believed that entrepreneurs are rare yet indispensable individuals who in fact make the economy work. Furthermore, he wrote that human contribution to economic growth came in three types: (1) scientists (who should respect that values are subjected to human will, abilities and needs, as they are within the domain of moral science), (2) workers (employer and employee are equally necessary to each other), and (3) entrepreneurs (to coordinate the other elements of production such as labour, capital and land, to produce products, estimate demand and market the product) (Barreto, 1989; Formaini, 2001: Rothbard, 1995; Schumpete, 1951).

Early English Views on the Entrepreneur

The first English term mimicking the French word *entrepreneur* appeared in the fifteenth century, as *adventurer,* to describe merchants operating at some risk, and then in the seventeenth century to describe land speculators, farmers and those who directed some public works. The word *adventurer* was replaced by the word *projector,* reflecting someone who was a cheat and a rogue (Hébert and Link, 2006).

Adam Smith, the Scottish philosopher and tax collector, quite often referred to as 'the economist' wrote *An Inquiry into the Nature and Causes of the Wealth of Nation* (1776), which is considered the origin of the entire British classical school of political economy. Smith (1776) had initially translated the word *entrepreneur* as *undertaker,* meaning 'one who undertakes a job or completes a project'. The concept evolved into that of government contractor, someone who, at his own financial risk, performed a task imposed on him by the government. The term was later extended to include those individuals who held exclusive franchises from the Crown or the Parliament: for example, tax farmers or persons commissioned to drain the fens. Over time, the government connection was dropped, and the term simply came to designate someone involved in a risky project from which an uncertain profit might be derived (Hoselitz, 1960). It is interesting to note that by the nineteenth century the word *undertaker* had acquired the special meaning of 'an arranger of funerals'. Eventually, *undertaker* was replaced by the term *entrepreneur* (Formaini, 2001; Hébert and Link, 1988; Rothbard, 1995; Smith, 1904).

English economists in this period used the term *undertaker* and omitted to use the French word *entrepreneur*. Some authors at the time claimed that Smith's view of the undertaker represented, in English terminology, the original Physiocratic entrepreneurial model. Others argued that Smith misrepresented Cantillon's work and neither understood nor used the entrepreneur concept at all. At the same time, his supporters maintained that 'production was a given', and therefore the roles of individual productive factors, which entrepreneurs are, needed no explanation. One may state that the early Physiocratic insights and extensions of Say (1803) were ignored during the classical period in England (Formaini, 2001; Hébert and Link, 1988; Rothbard, 1955; Smith, 1904).

It should also be observed that while some authors rejected any separate role for the entrepreneur, this title was replaced by the comprehensive term *capitalist,* the meaning of which was self-explanatory. The Latin origin of the word *capital* is *capitalis,* from the proto-Indo-European *kaput,* which means 'head', suggesting how wealth was measured. Adam Smith expresses his own favoured economic system as 'the system of natural liberty', while at the same time making the word *capital* central to the thinking of the political economy (Formaini, 2001: Rothbard, 1995: Smith, 1904).

1560 words

Here are some suggestions for improving your speed reading:
- Speed read emails. Use your mouse cursor as the guide. It works really well.
- Practise on materials you are not familiar with: for example, a mathematics, science or medical textbook. This will help you to create new visuals for words you don't know.

- Newspapers are also a great way to practise speed reading, as words are displayed in narrow columns. Using a guide will help you get through these much quicker and form a basis for good practice.
- Teach others. It will improve your understanding of speed reading.
- Speed reading is only an alternative way of reading, so don't think it needs to be a permanent replacement to your usual reading. If you feel like lying in bed reading a novel nice and slowly, by all means go for it. You are now equipped with a special skill that you can turn on at any given point.
- Comprehension will increase when you start visualising content in context (within the story). The more you practise visualisation, the more you are working towards stronger comprehension. Remember, comprehension is only the result of speed reading practice. You can't just 'do' comprehension. It has to be achieved. It's like going to the gym for a workout: you can't just get toned, you have to work at it.
- Enjoy speed reading. Play around, make mistakes and persist. After all, this is a learning process and it takes time — don't make it stressful. Without enjoyment, you may as well read as you normally would without any techniques.

Key Points

- Speed reading is really 'image reading'. Images are registered a lot faster in our brain than words. As in the Yellow Elephant model, the words are abstract and need to be converted to an image in order to make sense and be part of the story; association.
- Conscious competence, reading guides, chunking and image flow are the tools that assist you to speed read.
- Practice makes perfect.

Goal Setting

'A goal is a dream with
a deadline.'

— NAPOLEON HILL

We all have dreams and aspirations. At the start of each year, millions of people around the world set new resolutions. But these resolutions are often forgotten about by the end of the year. How many people do you know who have resolved to lose weight or quit smoking? There is a strong chance that most of these people were unable to achieve their goals. We have great intentions but many of us have trouble taking action to achieve our goals. In this chapter we look at a mind tool that will help you connect to your goals and generate motivation to achieve them: mind mapping. Mind mapping is a tool that can be used for any purposes — to introduce you to it, we look at its usefulness in goal setting.

If you are someone that never formally sets goals, it could mean that you have a strong vision of what you want to achieve and know how to go about it, or it could mean that you are not clear on your goals and do not know where to start. One way to get started is to use a mind map. Developed by Tony Buzan, mind mapping is a tool that uses both sides of the brain to engage with information. For a detailed explanation of mind mapping, I recommend *The Mind Map Book* by Tony Buzan.

Take the example of a student preparing notes for their studies. When I was studying at university, I would write at least eight pages of notes per lecture. If I went to twenty lectures in the semester, that's 20 × 8 (pages) and 160 pages of notes taken! That's lot of knowledge, which is great. However, I only looked at my notes when it was time to study hard for my exam — usually at the last minute. Like many students, I would cram for the exam by going through all my notes in an unstructured way, all one night. I did pass the exams, but not very well. Did I remember what I had learnt once my exams were over? Nope. It was party time! In the next semester, I'd start afresh with new subjects and apply the same old learning strategy. Not a very effective approach!

What happens with traditional note-taking is that important themes and concepts are not aligned. They may seem to be, as the notes are written in logical order, but in fact themes and concepts are scattered throughout. It's similar with books — often you can turn to the index at the back to find where particular topics are mentioned. It may indicate that a particular topic is discussed on pages 3, 4 and 238. You have to flick back and forth to find it. What mind mapping allows you to do is to gather all your topics, themes, concepts and so on, on the one page. It provides instant access to those topics, instead of having to go from page to page. You can also see how one topic (branch) relates to others. In contrast, if I write about a particular topic on page 3 of my study notes and about a similar issue on pages 7, 12 and 50, when I revise I may not see direct associations between them. However, if they are all on one branch, I will see the information I need precisely without having to sift through pages. Mind mapping provides an uninterrupted flow of information that can be easily followed.

Now let's see how mind mapping can help us in setting goals. To begin the goal setting process we begin by thinking about our overall goals. For example, in order for me to successfully memorise the telephone book, I had to first create the goal of memorising it, and then work out the strategy I would use to do so. The three-step mind-mapping strategy described below allowed me to do this in record time. You can take the same approach I did and apply it to any part of your life. Whether it be a career, financial or educational goal, the process will allow you to create clear paths as to how to achieve your goals.

The three-step process is simple and works like this:

1 LIST YOUR GOALS

List all your goals. They can be very specific, such as 'memorise the telephone book' or very broad, such as 'become the CEO of an organisation'. It doesn't matter at this stage. It is important to keep these goals as generic as possible. For example, instead of writing down a goal as 'improve reading comprehension', write down 'reading'. Then under the main branch of 'reading' create another branch for 'comprehension'. Now you can also add other branches to 'reading', such as

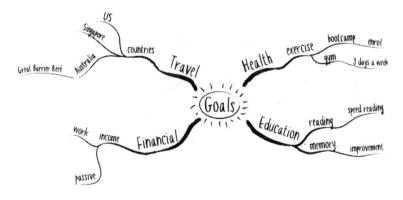

'speed' and 'read more'. The more generic you make the main branch, the more details you can add on smaller branches.

On the previous page is an example mind map of one person's personal goals.

2 CREATE AN ACTION LIST

Now that you have a list of goals and their subgoals, it is crucial to ask yourself the questions: How am I going to achieve this? What do I need to do to be able to achieve my goal? If you had 'reading' as your main goal, and a subgoal of 'comprehension', you will need to ask yourself how you will achieve greater reading comprehension. Add your answers as sub-branches from the 'comprehension' branch. There will always be an answer. If you don't know, think about what you could do to gain the knowledge or resource to do it. In this way, you will generate an action list of to-do items that you can check off. Creating action points provides you with a roadmap of the tasks required to get to your goal.

A mind map is dynamic enough that it will also help you think of tasks or ideas you may have missed or not added. For

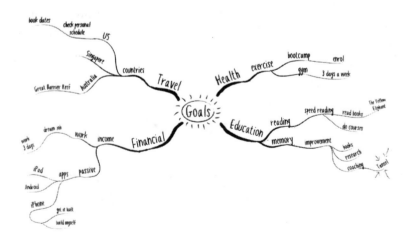

example, the mind map on the next page has 'exercise' as an action with two subheadings: 'bootcamp' and 'gymnasium'. I can add more branches underneath 'exercise', such as 'aerobics', 'football' and so on. This will not affect the structure of the mind map. I can also add further subheadings underneath, such as the specific type of exercise. You can always keep going: it is best to fill in as much as you can. This will help you identify many ways to achieve your goal. Also, identifying many small actions assists you in finding better pathways to your goal.

3 USE EMOTIVE WORDS AND IMAGES

So now you have your goals on a mind map. Ask yourself how you would feel once you have achieved them. Don't just write down 'good' or 'happy'. Imagine how cool it would be to be able to read a book in ten minutes and understand it better than before. Or to be able to remember the names of everyone you meet with no trouble whatsoever. How would you feel? What would be the exact word(s) to describe the feeling?

Visualise the moment of achievement and describe the exact emotions. The positive words you come up with should

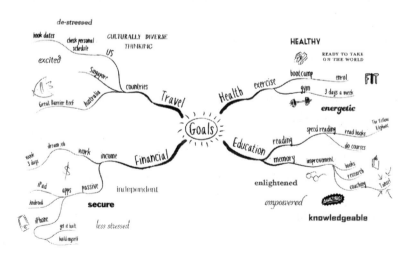

trigger positive emotions in you now. This can also motivate you to work harder on achieving your goals, as you want to revisit that visualised moment. Ask yourself how this awesome feeling would look. Try adding photos, drawings, clippings — whatever gives you a visual trigger to that feeling associated with achieving your goal. A picture is worth a thousand words.

Once you have completed the three-step mind map process for your goals, make sure you place your mind map somewhere you can see it often. You will want to be able to refer to it and keep adding further branches, pictures, experiences and so on. The more involved you are with your goals, the stronger the story in your head, which will in turn create more engagement and result in you working much more diligently to achieve them.

Remember that mind mapping can be used for many different purposes, not just goal setting. If you want to greatly improve your knowledge of what you read, then mind mapping provides a great way to further improve recall and comprehension.

Key Points

- Mind mapping draws on both the left and right sides of the brain, making it one of the most effective learning techniques available.
- Try mind mapping many topics to get used to the process. The more practice you get, the more effective you will become at structuring and organising information.
- Add images that inspire you or that remind you of the content of your mind map.
- Work hard on developing your action list. These are the tasks you need to complete to accomplish your main goals. Be open to new methods you haven't considered before.
- Enjoy the process! Think of all the great things you're looking forward to achieving.

Everyday Applications of Memory Techniques

Time moves in one direction, memory
in another.

WILLIAM GIBSON

Application of Techniques

'It was character that got us out of bed,
commitment that moved us into action, and
discipline that enabled us to follow through.'

— ZIG ZIGLAR

THIS CHAPTER SHOWS YOU some of the practical ways memory techniques can help you achieve your goals. You will discover ways to apply memory techniques to your own specific needs.

Remembering Names

Here's the scenario. You're invited to a function. It's a great event and lots of people introduce themselves to you. You hear their names but they barely register before you're introduced to more people. Later you find yourself talking to one person for some time and it suddenly hits you: you can't recall their name. Even more embarrassing is the fact that the other person is using your name comfortably in conversation. But all you can think to use in reply is 'mate', 'buddy' or 'bro'. You wait desperately in the hope that they will mention their name again or that someone will call out to them while you're talking. But it doesn't happen. What do you do?

There are various ways that you could handle this type of situation:

- Ask the person their name again and try and commit it to memory this time around. Most people won't do this and will try and hold out until they remember the person's name or hear it again.
- Ask for their business card if they have one. You can then pretend you knew their name all along by confidently using their name in conversation.
- Try and steer the conversation in a way to get the person to mention their name. This requires a lot of skill. It's not really worth the effort unless you want to test how good you are at manipulating conversation.
- Give your mobile phone to them to enter their name and number.

Of course all of this could have been avoided if you had used memory techniques to remember their name in the first place. This is the easiest method of all, as it means you can concentrate on the conversation and not worry about trying to remember a name.

Forgetting names, especially in business, can have a detrimental effect on relationships. Business is all about people. The better you connect, the better the business. And the first point of connection is usually a person's name. Getting it right and using it in conversation is a strong interpersonal skill. It tells the person hearing their name that they are valuable. It makes them feel special. Building rapport in this way is essential to business success.

Following are some strategies I use to help me remember names. These strategies have allowed me both to remember names in daily life and to set memory records for the Names and Faces category at memory championships around the world.

Rhyming or Sound-alike Word

Some names rhyme with or sound like other words, which can make them easier to remember. For instance, Kylie rhymes with 'smiley' and Peter with 'heater'. Tansel sounds like 'tinsel', 'tonsil' or 'utensil' — as you can imagine, I got teased quite a bit at school. Kids have amazing imaginations and are very inventive in the associations they make when teasing.

This trick to remembering a name through using a rhyming or similar sounding word is to make up a cool story using the VAI memory principle. For example, 'when I met Kylie, she was so *smiley* that her mouth stretched from one ear to the other, which made her look a bit freaky', or 'I met Peter, who was burning from standing too close to the *heater* in his not so woolly wind*cheater*'.

Someone You Know

If the name of the person you're meeting is the same as someone you already know, you can use this to build an association. For instance, say you meet an Amber and it just so happens that your cat's name is also Amber. Your association could be: 'my cat's name is Amber, so every time I meet an Amber, I imagine patting my cat'.

Mnemonic or Play on Words

Let's say you meet a Jemima. You can break her name down into 'jem miner': imagine the person you meet mining for gems. Using more difficult name, for example Wijesinghe (pronounced *vee-jay-sing-he*), you could turn it into 'DJ sing he'. So the story can be that the person you meet is a DJ singing. Who was singing? HE was.

Location

You meet someone named Shane. Do you know anyone named Shane? How about Shane Warne, the famous Aussie cricketer? In which location do you imagine Shane Warne? Quite possibly a cricket pitch. So when you meet a Shane, place them mentally on a cricket pitch, about to be struck by a cricket ball.

By making up silly stories, remembering names can become loads of fun. Practise these techniques and see how you go. The internet provides lots of opportunities for practising — you could go through your social media lists and memorise all the names in your Facebook, Twitter or LinkedIn accounts, if you have them.

Memorising Talks and Speeches

You may have heard the statistic that more people in the world fear public speaking than death. People are terrified to get up and talk in front of an audience. What if they forget something? What if they stuff it all up? What if they appear nervous, blush or shake? How would they be seen by the audience and by their peers? For many people, the thought of these things is worse than the fear of death. I still find it extraordinary when I run speaking workshops in organisations that so many people are afraid of what others will think of them.

Using memory techniques can help you destroy the fear of public humiliation. Not only that, but they can help you to create talks that are engaging, memorable and, most importantly, communicate messages that don't suck.

Some basic strategies are given on the following pages to help you remember your speech and be confident delivering your message.

Linking

Connect each major point of your presentation with a story using the VAI principle. Let's say your talk is about organisational vision and you structure it as follows:

1. Introduction
2. What our organisation is about
3. What our organisation has been doing
4. Our successes
5. Our vision
6. How we intend to get there
7. Your contribution
8. Questions
9. Thank you

For each of the topics, you have a number of information points and details. You prepare your speech in advance and know the topic you are talking about well. Once you have a good understanding of the material you wish to present, you next need to memorise the order of key points in your talk. You can do this by creating a story using visualisation, association and imagination.

You can imagine *introducing* yourself by bowing down so low you actually fall. This little drama will help you remember 'Introduction'. You get up from the fall and walk into your organisation and meet new staff. You are too excited about meeting new people to tell them *about your organisation.* They ask you a question about *what the organisation does* and you tell them the organisation has been helping people achieve great health. The new staff cheer with glee, saying *'great success!',* acknowledging the fine work done. In fact, one of the new staff leaps so high with excitement that her glasses fall off and shatter. Now she can't see and has no *vision.* You ask her how she *intends to get* to her car without her glasses. She says she doesn't know, and you kindly offer *your contribution* of taking her to her car. After you've left her, she *questions* herself, saying, 'Hang on, I'm in my car but I still can't see!' Her friend pops out from the corner and says, 'Here you go, I've just fixed your glasses; they are as good as new!' *'Thank you,'* says the lady.

Go through the story a few times, making it as visual as possible, then test yourself to make sure you can recall it.

Method of Loci

You can also use locations to help you memorise speeches. The advantage of using the Method of Loci is that you can add further subtopics of your talk if you need to. Let's take the example of a presentation about Melbourne and its weather for a tourism company. Using your house for the *loci,* you could imagine it experiencing all four seasons, and structure your talk as follows:

- **Bedroom:** Melbourne
  1. Introduction
  2. Raining
  3. Floods

- **Living room:** Melbourne in summer
  4. Heat waves
  5. Skin cancer prevention
  6. Natural disasters

- **Study:** Other states
  7. Weather across different states
  8. Victoria
  9. New South Wales

- **Kitchen:** Conclusion
  10. Weather in Australia is temperamental

11. However, when it's nice there's nothing like it
12. Come visit Australia!

To help you memorise the subtopics for each rooms, link them with particular features in the room. For example:

- *Locus* 4 (couch) — The couch was set on fire by the heat waves.
- *Locus* 5 (TV) — If you touch the TV screen with your skin you can get skin cancer.
- *Locus* 6 (coffee table) — The coffee table was burnt down by a huge wall of fire.

Memorise the above twelve points in this way, then test yourself to see if you can recall them.

Memorising Book Contents

Want to know what a book is all about without having to read all of it? Here's a cool way of using mind mapping to grasp the content of a book. It doesn't take long and can even be done without speed reading.

I call this the keyword map. It can be applied to a whole book or a section of a book, such as a chapter. Here's how it works.

1 SPEED READ CHAPTER

Use a reading guide and read in images as you go through the content. Forming images is crucial so that you have pictures in your head with which you can build further associations.

2 IDENTIFY KEYWORDS

As you are speed reading, write down or underline the important words. This will help you to visualise and develop a logical sequence of keywords.

3 MIND MAP KEYWORDS

Once you have finished reading, create a mind map using the keywords you identified. If you find this difficult, repeat steps 1 and 2 again. You will find once you start mind mapping that it gets easier and easier to see how keywords fit onto branches to create a pattern of information. Practise regularly and you'll soon find it comes easily.

4 ADD OWN KNOWLEDGE AND EXPERIENCE

Once you have finished your mind map, you may be able to expand it by adding related knowledge or ideas from other sources — perhaps you have experience with the particular topic or it reminds you of something else. Doing this will create greater emotional connection with your mind map, thus involving you more deeply in your own learning.

I've used this process when studying, and it has saved me lots of time. I am expected to complete around three to four hours of reading a week for each subject at university. If I do three subjects in a semester, that's twelve hours of reading. However, using speed reading, keywords and mind mapping, I could complete all my reading for all subjects in around two hours.

An even greater benefit is that my notes take up much less space. I don't end up with hundreds of pages of notes, as happens for so many students. If one subject has thirteen lectures, I simply end up with thirteen mind maps full of knowledge.

Practise by making a keyword map of the passage below.

Ubuntu Culture

KYLIE HARKER

Pulling Together as One

Successful business leaders are passionate about growing their organisations; they want real success and enjoyment from both their business and their personal lives.

Every organisation has a range of capabilities that are realised through the resources at its disposal, such as systems and equipment. However, its ability to function at its peak is dictated by the people who operate those systems, equipment and other resources. This presents a challenge if the people are disengaged with the company on any level.

Engaging People's Brilliance

The ability of the leader to create a burning desire or passion for peak performance in their people is the key. Furthermore, for a company to develop massive momentum, individuals need to have an interest in helping others around them also perform at their best.

Creating a high-performance culture is not just about leaders inspiring and helping their people to excel. It is also about harnessing the collective skills and wisdom of the organisation and galvanising employees to help others perform at their best.

So how do we engage our people to perform at their best as often as possible?

The answer: create an Ubuntu culture.

Ubuntu is an ancient African philosophy. Put simply, it means 'I am because we are' or 'my success is bound in your success'. This kind of culture brings people together to achieve goals that would be impossible as individuals.

The overall feeling it creates is 'we're all in this together'.

When your people genuinely understand how their individual role and performance affects the ability of the whole team to achieve the organisation's collective goals, you have the key to unlocking considerable momentum and making people joyful and engaged.

An organisation with Ubuntu at its core consists of people who connect in meaningful ways, are affirming of others, harness the collective wisdom and use it to achieve amazing results.

Ubuntu leaders know that inspiring and helping others to be the best they can be is the only way to elevate their own success and that of the organisation. An Ubuntu team instinctively knows that together they can achieve more than the disparate parts. Like a pride of lions hunting a buffalo they move as one in an agile and dynamic fashion with a mindset that empowers them to confidently take on projects far bigger than they would on their own or as a single department.

Developing the Tools

Crucial to creating an Ubuntu culture is clarifying what the collective is trying to achieve and what each person's role in it is.

This means being crystal clear on three areas:

Core purpose: Why does the organisation do what it does? What is its Reason for Being? Often little more than a three-word statement, this kind of clarity gives people a way of navigating decisions in a very deliberate and potent manner. A terrific example would be Walt Disney's 'Make People Happy'.

Vision: People need to know what they are moving towards, if a company does not have a clear and compelling vision of what they are growing into, good people will leave or burn out and the people who remain will slowly dilute the organisation's effectiveness and brand.

Culture: There needs to be clarity about what appropriate values and behaviours are and how these align with the organisation's purpose and vision. Once defined, it is easy to identify specific behaviours that indicate people are acting in alignment with the organisation's culture. If they are not acting in this way, it is easier to spot and remedy.

Creating a Cultural Blueprint ('this is how we are' document)

Leaders often talk about 'culture' but rarely determine what tangible behaviours will enable it.

What's required is a blueprint of the kind of culture that will achieve the core purpose of the organisation. This needs to state clearly how the values of the company will affect the people who are a part of it and those who interact with it, such as clients. Clear, tangible behaviours should be mapped out so people understand what is expected of them; they can then be held accountable in a very powerful way.

However, the ability to develop this blueprint and lead people accordingly requires a specific mindset and skillset. As a leader, you must embody the organisation's values and take intelligent and deliberate actions to ensure what you develop comes 'alive' within the organisation.

This can be done by designing carefully crafted touchpoints that will enable employees to experience the purpose, vision and culture in a very real way. For instance, an organisation whose core purpose is 'Ignite the Desire to Learn' may provide tailored learning and external education opportunities for its employees.

You will also need to decide how the company culture will be exhibited by leaders at meetings, birthday celebrations, social functions and performance reviews.

Harnessing Collective Skills and Wisdom

The Ubuntu leader has the mindset and skills to harness the collective energy and wisdom of their people.

This starts by having conversations with your people, getting to know them personally, finding out what's important to them outside of work, what they do in their spare time and what aspirations they have. To do this, you need to be among them on a daily basis, recall what's going well and what's important in their world.

By engaging with your people in an authentic manner, you will create a sense of connection that allows for natural, comfortable conversations free from the fear of judgement. These social interactions — be they lunchroom conversations, water cooler chats or conversations at a social event — will provide you with insights and snippets of information you would not ordinarily come across. They will also provide you with a much greater understanding of your people, who they really are and what inspires and matters to them.

These conversations will also empower your people and help unleash their creative thought processes, resulting in innovative ideas and practices.

By getting to know your people, you are also given the opportunity to tap into their personal passions. People want to be presented with opportunities to learn and be challenged. Ask them what they want for themselves and how they see themselves contributing to the organisation. Find ways to incorporate their passions and talents in a way that support and achieves the greater vision. For example, an employee with a passion for gardening could bring untold value to a company that operates childcare centres. Just imagine the garden oasis they could create for the children to play in or the vegetable patch that would enable wonderful education opportunities about food sourcing.

An Ubuntu culture takes into account everyone's experiences and benefits from them. Rather than hoarding ideas and strategies, you harness the collective wisdom of the organisation by creating an environment that values the sharing of knowledge among team members — an environment where people's conversations are encouraged and listened to.

Ubuntu leaders don't shy away from thoughtful, challenging discussions in group or team meetings. They embrace them because they know they will lead to innovative ideas and initiatives that everyone can be a part of. Feedback is specific, immediate and delivered contextually.

In these meetings, leaders should be asking questions that magnify the good such as: 'What's gone well for you guys? How did you achieve that?' Ubuntu leaders know that this could result in the team collectively deciding how that experience and resultant strategy could be used in other areas of the organisation.

In this way, everyone is given the opportunity to contribute their unique talents and the best of themselves. Other team members can develop skills, model best practice and learn the most effective strategies from each other without being fearful that another's success diminishes their own.

Ubuntu Leads to Authentic Success

The ultimate goal for an Ubuntu leader is authentic success. This is a lifestyle of making decisions with a clear understanding of what feels sustainably good. It is not ruthless business but sustainably serving the greatest good. For members of a team, it is not personal glory but being part of something bigger.

So the challenge for today's leader is to seek ways to engage their people, nurture their abilities, and align them to a common purpose and vision. The power of linking personal, professional and organisational goals brings people together in a collaborative way that unleashes success. An Ubuntu culture breeds great results and launches authentic success on multiple fronts for people and the organisations they belong to.

Ubuntu creates a sense of unity, teamwork and collaboration that is often missing from organisations. This approach has the power to transform our organisations. And reshape both our personal and our professional relationship.

The question that begins this journey for any leader is 'How can I help others to be great?'

1458 words

Studying

Millions of students out there do not have a strategy for learning and studying. They simply turn up to class, listen passively to the teacher or lecturer and repeat the cycle. How many people do you know who can't remember what they studied at school or university, even though they passed their courses? It is a common occurrence, even at the highest level of study.

This presents a perception problem. For example, a workplace sees the wonderful qualifications someone has on their CV and assumes they are competent in what they've learnt. The grades confirm this. However, grades only assess the knowledge for the particular moment in time. The student could have crammed the knowledge all in one night. Once the assessment was finished, the student was not obligated to learn any further. Why should they? After all, they obtained their degree, right?

The three-step study process I have developed below will help you enjoy the learning process and take more in.

1 PRE-STUDY

You will usually be required to do some reading for your studies. If not, then nothing is stopping you from obtaining relevant materials and engaging in this process proactively. Technology makes this a lot simpler, as many institutions provide lecture notes or PowerPoint slides. In the pre-study stage, speed read as much of the available material as you can and create keyword maps for what you read, either electronically or by hand.

2 DURING STUDY

Class time should be all about listening actively and being involved. If you're taking notes like crazy, you will be somewhat distracted from the learning process. It's much better to listen actively. While listening, use the VAI memory principle to visualise what is being said. Create images in your head with which you can, in turn, build associations. Have any relevant keyword maps from your pre-study reading in front of you. Since you have read the materials, the lecture will make more sense and hence you can add keywords and points from the lecture directly to the mind map. Your mind map will be enhanced, with all the relevant points still on one page.

3 POST-STUDY

Most people don't generally review or look back over their notes after taking them. Even when they do, it's usually just a quick glance to get the main points. This post-study step allows you to solidify your learning and complete your mind map for that particular lecture or study topic. Over time, fill out the mind map you developed in the lecture or class with any extra bits of knowledge you come across. Adding your own experiences to the mind map also helps, as any stories you can add engage your mind and help you remember.

X	2	3	4	5	6	7	8	9	10	11	12
2	hair	hatch	hoof	doze	dine	door	DJ	Daffy	nose	nun	Nero
3	hatch	hoop	dine	dale	Daffy	wand	Nero	nike	mouse	ma'am	MJ
4	hoof	dine	DJ	nose	Nero	knife	money	MJ	rose	roar	reef
5	toes	dale	nose	nail	mouse	mail	rose	rail	loose	lily	cheese
6	dine	Daffy	Nero	mouse	MJ	Arnie	reef	lawyer	cheese	cha-cha	gun
7	door	net	knife	mail	Arnie	ruby	leech	chime	agassi	cake	fur
8	DJ	Nero	money	rose	reef	leech	chair	gun	vase	fife	peach
9	Daffy	nike	MJ	rail	lawyer	chime	gun	fat	bass	babe	adhesive
10	nose	mouse	rose	loose	cheese	agassi	vase	bass	daisies	dates	tent
11	nun	ma'am	roar	lily	cha-cha	cake	fife	babe	dates	tent	demon
12	Nero	MJ	reef	cheese	gun	fur	peach	adhesive	dance	demon	drier

There is now a well formed knowledge base all on one page for that particular topic. Importantly, it is not a huge wad of pages: it's concise and memorable. If you do this for all classes, you'll find it easy to store the notes for future reference.

Memorising the Times Tables

In school, you probably remember learning the times tables — an essential part of the school curriculum. Even as an adult, recalling them is very useful as we all work with numbers in some form or another.

Using the Major system, we are able to memorise times tables without heavy repetition. This is also a fun way to help engage your kids with mathematics. Using the Times Tables Story Matrix on the following page, you can make up a story for each equation, using the corresponding images for the numbers. For example:

10 (toes) × 4 (hair) = 40 (rose)

Then make up a story using these images: 'Your TOES get larger and larger and a horse passes by and steps on your HAIR with its massive hoof. As a result, you start to cry. The horse feels bad and gives you a ROSE.'

The answer will reveal itself as a result of what happened in your story — you just need to convert the final image (rose) back into the corresponding number (40).

Let's look at another example:

9 (hoop) × 8 (hoof) = 72 (can)

The story could be: 'The horse was playing around with a hula-HOOP and accidently tripped, and its HOOF fell off. As a result, it turned around and found a CAN with which to bang its hoof back in again.'

The stories can be as silly as you like. Children love making them up! What about numbers outside the Times Table Story Matrix? The Major system can still be applied. In fact, it can be applied to any number. For example:

12 (tin) × 35 (mail) = 420 (rains — from the Major system, 4 = r, 2 = n, 0 = s)

The story could be: 'You put your hand in your MAILbox only to find a piece of TIN. You had no idea what it was for, so you threw it up in the air. It went up so high it brought in the RAINS.'

Here's a mind challenge for you. See if you can recall the answers to the equations given below by creating stories using the Major system to translate the answers.

1. 93 × 38 = 3534
2. 27 × 87 = 2349
3. 13 × 54 = 702
4. 32 × 67 = 2144
5. 72 × 21 = 1512
6. 49 × 43 = 2107
7. 88 × 17 = 1496
8. 31 × 55 = 1705
9. 47 × 52 = 2444
10. 92 × 78 = 7176
11. 70 × 65 = 4550
12. 25 × 85 = 2125
13. 62 × 19 = 1178
14. 89 × 44 = 3916
15. 74 × 23 = 1702
16. 99 × 53 = 5247
17. 18 × 48 = 864
18. 33 × 16 = 528
19. 432 × 67 = 28,944
20. 321 × 978 = 313,938

Memorising the Periodic Table of Elements

Charts of the periodic table are commonly stuck on walls in science classrooms and chemistry labs, but the table is just not easy to remember! The Method of Loci is a useful way to memorise all 118 elements, one after the other. Once we have done that, we can then associate them with the symbol, meaning and whatever else we'd like to memorise.

You will first require 118 locations. Next, convert each atomic number to an image, using the Major system. Once you have your image, use the VAI principle to make it stand out in your head. If you want to remember the atomic numbers, symbols and origins of the names, associate your visual representation with these as well. Or you could just remember the elements. Either way provides good practice at using your imagination skills along with the Method of Loci.

For example: 'As I was drinking TEA (1), WATER started to form on top of it and it made the shape of a letter H.'

See if you can memorise all 118 elements, along with their atomic number, symbol and origin of name.

Atomic number	Element	Symbol	Origin of name
1	Hydrogen	H	the Greek *hydro* and *genes*, meaning 'water-forming'
2	Helium	He	the Greek *helios*, meaning 'sun'
3	Lithium	Li	the Greek *lithos*, meaning 'stone'
4	Beryllium	Be	the Greek name for 'beryl', *beryllo*
5	Boron	B	the Arabic *buraq*, which was the name for borax
6	Carbon	C	the Latin *carbo*, meaning 'charcoal'
7	Nitrogen	N	the Greek *nitron* and genes, meaning 'nitre-forming'
8	Oxygen	O	the Greek *oxy* and *genes*, meaning 'acid-forming'
9	Fluorine	F	the Latin *fluere*, meaning 'to flow'
10	Neon	Ne	the Greek *neos*, meaning 'new'
11	Sodium	Na	the English word *soda* (*natrium* in Latin)

12	Magnesium	Mg	Magnesia, a district of Eastern Thessaly in Greece
13	Aluminium	Al	the Latin name for alum *alumen*, meaning 'bitter salt'
14	Silicon	Si	the Latin *silex or silicis*, meaning 'flint'
15	Phosphorus	P	the Greek *phosphoros*, meaning 'bringer of light'
16	Sulfur	S	either from the Sanskrit *sulvere*, or the Latin *sulfurium*, both names for sulphur
17	Chlorine	Cl	the Greek *chloros*, meaning 'greenish yellow'
18	Argon	Ar	the Greek *argos*, meaning 'idle'
19	Potassium	K	the English word *potash* (*kalium* in Latin)
20	Calcium	Ca	the Latin *calx*, meaning 'lime'
21	Scandium	Sc	Scandinavia (from the Latin name *Scandia*)
22	Titanium	Ti	Titans, the sons of the Earth goddess of Greek mythology
23	Vanadium	V	Vanadis, an old Norse name for the Scandinavian goddess Freyja
24	Chromium	Cr	the Greek *chroma*, meaning 'colour'
25	Manganese	Mn	either from the Latin *magnes*, meaning 'mangnet' or *magnesia nigra*, meaning 'black magnesium oxide'
26	Iron	Fe	the Anglo-Saxon name *iren* (*ferrum* in Latin)
27	Cobalt	Co	the German word *kobald*, meaning 'goblin'
28	Nickel	Ni	shortened form of the German *kupfernickel*, meaning either 'devil's copper' or 'St Nicholas's copper'
29	Copper	Cu	the Old English term *coper*, in turn derived from the Latin *Cyprium aes*, meaning 'a metal from Cyprus'

30	Zinc	Zn	the German *zinc*, which may in turn be derived from the Persian word *sing*, meaning 'stone'
31	Gallium	Ga	France (from the Latin name *Gallia*)
32	Germanium	Ge	Germany (from the Latin name *Germania*)
33	Arsenic	As	the Greek *arsenikon*, meaning 'the yellow pigment or piment'
34	Selenium	Se	the moon (from the Greek name *selene*)
35	Bromine	Br	the Greek *bromos*, meaning 'stench'
36	Krypton	Kr	the Greek *kryptos*, meaning 'hidden'
37	Rubidium	Rb	the Latin *rubidius*, meaning 'deepest red'
38	Strontium	Sr	Strontian, a small town in Scotland
39	Yttrium	Y	Ytterby, Sweden
40	Zirconium	Zr	the Persian *zargun*, meaning 'gold coloured'
41	Niobium	Nb	Niobe, daughter of king Tantalus from Greek mythology
42	Molybdenum	Mo	the Greek *molybdos* meaning 'lead'
43	Technetium	Tc	the Greek *tekhnetos*, meaning 'artificial'
44	Ruthenium	Ru	Russia (from the Latin name *Ruthenia*)
45	Rhodium	Rh	the Greek *rhodon*, meaning 'rose coloured'
46	Palladium	Pd	Athena (Pallas Athena), the goddess of wisdom from Greek mythology
47	Silver	Ag	the Anglo-Saxon name *siolfur* (*argentum* in Latin)
48	Cadmium	Cd	the Latin name for the mineral calmine: cadmia
49	Indium	In	the Latin *indicium*, meaning 'violet' or 'indigo'

50	Tin	Sn	the Anglo-Saxon word *tin* (*stannum* in Latin, meaning 'hard')
51	Antimony	Sb	the Greek *anti-monos*, meaning 'not alone' (*stibium* in Latin)
52	Tellurium	Te	Earth, the third planet in the solar system (from the Latin word *tellus*)
53	Iodine	I	the Greek *iodes*, meaning 'violet'
54	Xenon	Xe	the Greek *xenos*, meaning 'stranger'
55	Caesium	Cs	the Latin *caesius*, meaning 'sky blue'
56	Barium	Ba	the Greek *barys*, meaning 'heavy'
57	Lanthanum	La	the Greek *lanthanein*, meaning 'to lie hidden'
58	Cerium	Ce	Ceres, the Roman God of agriculture
59	Praseodymium	Pr	the Greek *prasios didymos*, meaning 'green twin'
60	Neodymium	Nd	the Greek *neos didymos*, meaning 'new twin'
61	Promethium	Pm	Prometheus of Greek mythology, who stole fire from the gods and gave it to humans
62	Samarium	Sm	Samarskite, the name of the mineral from which it was first isolated
63	Europium	Eu	Europe
64	Gadolinium	Gd	Johan Gadolin, chemist, physicist and mineralogist
65	Terbium	Tb	Ytterby, Sweden
66	Dysprosium	Dy	the Greek *dysprositos*, meaning 'hard to get'
67	Holmium	Ho	Stockholm, Sweden (with the Latin name *Holmia*)
68	Erbium	Er	Ytterby, Sweden
69	Thulium	Tm	Thule, the ancient name for Scandinavia
70	Ytterbium	Yb	Ytterby, Sweden

71	Lutetium	Lu	Paris, France (with the Roman name *Lutetia*)
72	Hafnium	Hf	Copenhagen, Denmark (with the Latin name *Hafnia*)
73	Tantalum	Ta	King Tantalus, father of Niobe from Greek mythology
74	Tungsten	W	the Swedish *tung sten* meaning 'heavy stone' (W is *wolfram*, the old name of the tungsten mineral wolframite)
75	Rhenium	Re	Rhine, a river that flows from Grisons in the eastern Swiss Alps to the North Sea coast in the Netherlands (with the Latin name *Rhenia*)
76	Osmium	Os	the Greek *osme*, meaning smell
77	Iridium	Ir	Iris, the Greek goddess of the rainbow
78	Platinum	Pt	the Spanish *platina*, meaning 'little silver'
79	Gold	Au	the Anglo-Saxon word *gold* (*aurum* in Latin, meaning 'glow of sunrise')
80	Mercury	Hg	Mercury, the first planet in the solar system (Hg from the former name *hydrargyrum*, which was from the Greek *hydr* — water — and *argyros* — silver)
81	Thallium	Tl	the Greek *thallos*, meaning 'a green twig'
82	Lead	Pb	the Anglo-saxon *lead* (*plumbum* in Latin)
83	Bismuth	Bi	the German *Bisemutum*, a corruption of *Weisse Masse*, meaning 'white mass'
84	Polonium	Po	Poland, the native country of Marie Curie, who first isolated the element
85	Astatine	At	the Greek *astatos*, meaning 'unstable'
86	Radon	Rn	from *radium*, as it was first detected as an emission from radium during radioactive decay

87	Francium	Fr	France
88	Radium	Ra	the Latin *radius,* meaning 'ray'
89	Actinium	Ac	the Greek *actinos,* meaning 'a ray'
90	Thorium	Th	Thor, the Scandinavian god of thunder
91	Protactinium	Pa	the Greek *protos,* meaning 'first', as a prefix to the element *actinium,* which is produced through the radioactive decay of protactinium
92	Uranium	U	Uranus, the seventh planet in the solar system
93	Neptunium	Np	Neptune, the eighth planet in the solar system
94	Plutonium	Pu	Pluto, a dwarf planet in the solar system
95	Americium	Am	Americas, the continent where the element was first synthesised
96	Curium	Cm	Pierre Curie, a physicist, and Marie Curie, a physicist and chemist
97	Berkelium	Bk	Berkeley, California, United States, where the element was first synthesised
98	Californium	Cf	State of California, United States, where the element was first synthesised
99	Einsteinium	Es	Albert Einstein, physicist
100	Fermium	Fm	Enrico Fermi, physicist
101	Mendelevium	Md	Dmitri Mendeleyev, chemist and inventor
102	Nobelium	No	Alfred Nobel, chemist, engineer, innovator and armaments manufacturer
103	Lawrencium	Lr	Ernest O Lawrence, Physicist
104	Rutherfordium	Rf	Ernest Rutherford, chemist and physicist
105	Dubnium	Db	Dubna, Russia
106	Seaborgium	Sg	Glenn T Seaborg, scientist
107	Bohrium	Bh	Niels Bohr, physicist

108	Hassium	Hs	Hesse, Germany, where the element was first synthesised
109	Meitnerium	Mt	Lise Meitner, physicist
110	Darmstadtium	Ds	Darmstadt, Germany, where the element was first synthesised
111	Roentgenium	Rg	Wilhelm Conrad Rontgen, physicist
112	Copernicium	Cn	Nicolaus Copernicus, astronomer
113	Ununtrium	Uut	IUPAC systematic element name
114	Flerovium	Fl	Georgy Flyorov, physicist
115	Ununpentium	Uup	IUPAC systematic element name
116	Livermorium	Lv	Lawrence Livermore National Laboratory, within the city of Livermore, California. United States, which collaborated with JINR on the discovery of the element
117	Ununseptium	Uus	IUPAC systematic element name
118	Ununoctium	Uuo	IUPAC systematic element name

Memorising Playing Cards

Besides being a cool party trick, memorising randomly shuffled playing cards enables you to practise using the VAI memory principle and improve your story making abilities. It is a great way of applying memory step 3 — association, from the Yellow Elephant model, as you can practise over and over again by shuffling the cards. Just follow the steps below.

1 CREATE IMAGES FOR PLAYING CARDS USING THE MAJOR SYSTEM

Each playing card is represented by an image. The image is created by using the Major system. The table on the next page shows how the images have been derived using the Major system column on the far left. You can either use my peg words or create your own.

Major system number	Spades	Clubs	Hearts	Diamonds
1 = T or D	A = seat	A = cat	A = hat	A = date
2 = N	2 = sun	2 = cone	2 = hen	2 = den
3 = M	3 = sumo	3 = cam	3 = ham	3 = dam
4 = R	4 = sir	4 = car	4 = hair	4 = deer
5 = L	5 = sail	5 = coal	5 = hail	5 = doll
6 = SH, CH, J, DG	6 = sash	6 = cash	6 = hatch	6 = DJ
7 = K, G, C, CK	7 = sack	7 = cake	7 = hook	7 = duck
8 = F or V	8 = safe	8 = coffee	8 = hoof	8 = Daffy
9 = P or B	9 = soap	9 = cap	9 = hoop	9 = tape
10 = S, Z	10 = sauce	10 = case	10 = hose	10 = toes
11 = DD, TT, DT, TD	J = sated	J = gutted	J = hated	J = dated
12 = TN, DN	Q = Satan	Q = kitten	Q = heathen	Q = Titan
13 = TM, DM	K = spade	K = club	K = heart	K = diamond

2 DEVELOP A FIFTY-TWO-*LOCI* JOURNEY

Write out fifty-two *loci* around your own house. Here are some suggestions.

1. front gate	2. front door	3. bed	4. shower
5. toilet	6. sink	7. cupboard	8. door
9. table	10. window	11. television	12. couch
13. coffee table	14. painting	15. vase	16. picture frame
17. plant	18. garage	19. pantry	20. fridge
21. oven	22. microwave	23. rubbish bin	24. stove
25. toaster	26. tap	27. dishwasher	28. kitchen bench
29. flowers	30. mirror	31. kitchen table	32. laptop
33. rose-bed	34. door	35. phone	36. lamp
37. bookshelf	38. drawers	39. desk	40. posters
41. whiteboard	42. computer	43. patio	44. trampoline
45. tree	46. shed	47. vegetable garden	48. cat beds
49. barbeque	50. toys	51. plants	52. side gate

3 MEMORISE CARDS ONTO THE FIFTY-TWO-*LOCI* JOURNEY

As you draw cards from the deck, use your *loci* from step 2 and make up a story with the card you draw for each location. For example: 'The HEN (2 of hearts) was making a really annoying "cluck cluck" sound at the front gate (*locus* 1). Someone threw a SEAT (ace of spades) through the front door (*locus* 2).'

Take a whole deck of cards, shuffle them so that they are random, place the cards face down and then pick up a card and associate it with a location. Fill in the rest of the table with the cards that you draw to memorise.

1. front gate / 2 of Hearts	2. front door / Ace of Spades	3. bed / 7 of Clubs	4.
5.	6.	7.	8.
9.	10.	11.	12.
13.	14.	15.	16.
17.	18.	19.	20.
21.	22.	23.	24.
25.	26.	27.	28.
29.	30.	31.	32.
33.	34.	35.	36.
37.	38.	39.	40.
41.	42.	43.	44.
45.	46.	47.	48.
49.	50.	51.	52.

Delivering Effective Presentations

Now that you understand how memory and learning work and you are familiar with basic principles and techniques, you can deliver far more effective presentations. The first step is to kill our old friend, Death by PowerPoint!

Keep your presentation simple and to the point. This allows the listener to develop quick visuals while practising step 3 — association. Einstein said that if you can't explain it simply, you don't understand it well enough. Focus on how you can best explain something using visualisation and association in a simple way. If you are inexperienced, you may initially find it difficult to shorten what you're trying to say, but mind mapping will help you with this.

Not everyone learns and understands the same way. When talking about something, try and use metaphors and stories. This gets the audience into association mode. Stories are much easier to remember. However, if the audience is more left-brained, it can also help to use numbers or logic behind what you're discussing. Think about who you are addressing.

Use images rather than words to make your points on PowerPoint slides. A classic example would be using a picture of a globe instead of writing 'we will become the top global distributor in the world'. The image will prompt you to explain what it signifies.

Focus on *how* you present. Body language accounts for 87 per cent of communication. So, if you're delivering a message, think about what are you doing with your body. How are you standing? What are you wearing? Where are you looking? The best communicators in the world are the ones who are in tune with their body when presenting to an audience. They know precisely how to align themselves to build rapport. Many inexperienced speakers fidget, say 'um' and 'ah', keep their hands in their pockets and stare only at the bullet points during the presentation. However, when I conduct public speaking workshops in organisations, by the end of the workshops people are more relaxed and enthusiastic, with a noticeable difference in body posture and language. Learning some memory strategies so that you can be confident you will remember your speeches without using notes can make all the difference.

Listening to Remember

I can honestly say that the biggest challenge for me growing up, in terms of memory, was remembering what was said in a conversation or what someone had told me. Lectures, classes and seminars did not interest me, as what was said went in one ear and out the other.

The strategy to use for listening effectively is the VAI memory principle. Begin by making up images for what people are saying — you need to be able to do this well before moving to the next part of the process. You can practise by using any audio source that you can find on the internet. Close your eyes and visualise what you hear, using your imagination. Once you feel comfortable with this step, try and associate what is being said with your image. For example, if I'm listening to the news radio and they are talking about a local petrol pump being robbed, I can imagine a petrol pump I personally know well, with people dressed up in superhero costumes, let's say as Batman, going in and producing a weapon, in this case a yoyo, and threatening the young man working there, requesting cash.

As silly as this sounds, it creates a visual in your mind. The story doesn't matter. I will only trigger the main point that the petrol pump was robbed. All you have done is accentuated the story and exaggerated it in your mind. The exaggeration will function as a prompt to the real (serious) story of a petrol pump robbery.

Try practising your VAI skill for listening in this way while listening to the daily news.

Learning Languages

Memory techniques can also be used to learn languages. As I've mentioned earlier, repetition can be stressful, but it's unfortunately the most common way of learning languages. Developing another way to learn, using both sides of our brain, makes it more fun and interesting. We can memorise the words in another language using the Major system and making up stories, which creates an image that in turn can create a story. For example, *gel* in Turkish means 'come here'. In English, *gel* means a mostly liquid form of substance. To remember the word in Turkish, you can make a story that connects the two meanings: you call someone over really loudly and then put *gel* in their hair as they approach you.

Developing a Habit Plan

'We are what we repeatedly do. Excellence, then, is not an act, but a habit.'

— ARISTOTLE

LEARNING MEMORY TECHNIQUES is one thing, but applying them in everyday life is another. Life can get extremely busy. So how do you practise what you've learnt in the limited time available? The answer is to develop a habit plan.

A habit plan is a process that enables you to create a set of tasks for using your new-found skill, so that you practise using them within the restrictions of your daily life.

To develop a habit plan:

1. Write down all the things you do during the day. I call these the 'work functions'. Work functions could include attending meetings, making phone calls, designing, negotiating, bricklaying, and so on. Whatever it is that constitutes a work task for you, write it down.
2. For each of your work functions, write down the process you are undertaking. If the function is emailing, then write

down 'typing' (emails) and 'reading' (emails). Even though these things may seem dead obvious, write them down, as they serve a greater purpose later on.

3. Once you have written down each of the processes you undertake for your work functions, think about the techniques you have learnt in this book and how they can assist you with those processes. For example, if you 'listen' when you are in a meeting, what could you do to enhance that listening?

An example of a habit plan is given below:

Work function	Processes	New techniques for applications
Attending meetings	Creating an agenda Taking notes Listening Contributing to discussion	Mind mapping VAI memory principle
Presenting	Writing and constructing the talk Memorising the talk Creating PowerPoints Delivery/communication	Mind mapping Method of Loci
Emailing	Reading Responding Organising	Speed reading
Travelling to work	Driving Bus Train	Visualising your day Speed reading documents Memorising playing cards

Writing down the new techniques or applications you will use in each situation will provide you with many opportunities to practise your new memory skill. Although new techniques may not be suitable for all the processes involved in your work functions, you will increasingly find, as you practise and improve your memory, that you start to think more creatively.

This will then assist you to add more approaches to your habit plan.

Key Points

- List as many work functions as you can.
- Add non-work functions as well.
- Make sure you carry out your new technique approaches.
- New technique approaches are not set in stone. Try them and if they require adjusting or a better strategy, simply change them as you go.
- The techniques do not have to be applied 100 per cent of the time. Work your way through them slowly and build the habit up.

Brain Training and
Putting Your Memory to Test

History is a people's memory, and without a memory,
man is demoted to the lower animals.

MALCOLM X

Ultimate Brain Training

> 'The brain is a wonderful organ; it starts working the moment you get up in the morning and does not stop until you get into the office.'
>
> — ROBERT FROST

As I MENTIONED EARLIER, we know how to exercise physically, but we don't often do much to exercise mentally. Memory training is the ultimate brain training, as it directly engages both sides of the brain to maximise creativity.

Memory training can help people from all walks of life. For example, training your memory for business will keep you creative and mindful. It will help you react a lot quicker in situations that require problem solving and decision-making, as the brain now has more ideas. You will also find yourself more conscious of these strategies when dealing with people. This can help you:

- make customer service or client relationships more memorable
- make training and learning in organisations more effective
- build rapport and know how to tell a story so that your audience knows exactly what you're trying to communicate.

By training your memory, which in turn trains your brain, you'll be able to do these things more quickly and easily.

As a mental athlete, memory training not only helps me to remember, but also keeps me focused and concentrated, which means I have all my attention on the task at hand and can perform to the best of my ability. Memory training can also help you in sports, as visualisation strategies can help you to throw, pass or score a goal more effectively. For example, if a footballer has the ball and is about to pass it off, instead of having maybe one or two options in their head for a split second, memory training can increase their mental capacity so they have six or seven possible ways of doing something effective with the ball. As a keen sportsperson I've used visualisation strategies along with memory techniques such as the VAI principle many times and it has allowed me to improve my playing. The opposition has been surprised by the unpredictability of the play.

The memory training exercises below have been specifically designed to work on all areas of brain function to help you become mentally fit and firing. Practise hard! Once you get into it, you will find you have better concentration, focus, mental agility and creativity. As you progress, challenge yourself by going faster and harder, just as you would with physical training.

Speed Reading Exercises
Quick Chunking

Exercise: Chunk faster without pausing too long on a group of words.

If you're using chunking as your speed-reading method of choice, practise mental strength by improving your speed of chunking. The quick chunks will allow you to eliminate pauses in your reading as you visualise images. This will also help you learn to move from step 1-abstract to step 2-image a lot faster.

Select one of the reading passages earlier in the book, and challenge yourself to read it again, this time chunking faster. Time yourself so you can see how you improve over time.

Five Seconds Per Page

Exercise: Read at a pace of five seconds per page, and use the keyword map tool to record what you read.

You will find that this exercise will allow you to summarise a whole chapter and get quite a bit of information out of it in only minutes. Taking five seconds to read a page means scanning or skim reading, rather than speed reading. So why read at this speed? The idea is to get an overview of what the page is about. In one of my speed reading workshops I had a participant from a Turkish background. English was his second language. I gave him a book on how to learn Japanese. I got him to read a chapter of around thirty pages, in five seconds per page. He finished it in two to three minutes. I then got him to complete a keyword map of the chapter. When it was his turn to present about what he had read, he described in detail what the chapter was about and he even went on to describe what some of the words meant. All this is three minutes of scanning and using the keyword map too! I have seen similar results in workshops from people of all ages, professions and walks of life.

Choose a book you are interested in and open it to the first chapter. With a clock or stopwatch beside you, begin reading, taking five seconds per page to scan as much as you can. You can use a reading prompt if it helps you. Scan from the top of the page to the bottom. I generally move my eyes in a zigzag pattern but you may find another method that works for you.

Speed Guide

Exercise: Move your reading guide a lot faster than you normally would. This challenges your brain to catch up to where you're pointing the guide.

The aim of this exercise is to train your brain to see more words at a time and increase your field of view when speed reading. By increasing your field of view, you will be able to view more words at a time and create images for what you are reading a lot more easily. Thus you will be able to read faster.

Select one of the reading passages earlier in the book, and challenge yourself to read it again, this time moving your reading guide more quickly. Time yourself so you can see how you improve over time.

Concentration

Exercise: Find your mental 'drain point' at your normal reading speed, then use speed reading to double it.

How long can you generally read for before you start to get mentally drained? If you hit the wall after ten minutes, then your challenge is to speed read for twenty minutes. If you get drained at twenty minutes, then try forty minutes of speed reading. This exercise is designed to help you build up concentration and remain focused.

Slow Speed Reading (Image Visualisation)

In this exercise, instead of reading a group of words in say, half a second, you deliberately read more slowly, taking possibly ten seconds per group of words but concentrating on the story you are building. This is quite a mentally strenuous exercise that works your capability to implement the VAI memory principle for reading. Do this well and you will find that you have increased comprehension when you return to a faster reading speed.

Forming images is a foundation of speed reading, allowing us to read more quickly because we naturally grasp images more quickly than words. This slow speed reading exercise focuses on your capacity to develop images that are clearer and have more depth.

For an extra challenge, try slow speed reading for twice as long as you usually would before hitting the brain drain point. This is what I call a 'mental boot camp'!

Memory Technique Exercises

The following exercises can be carried out while memorising either decks of cards in order or numbers in order. I have used the example of cards below, but the same brain training exercises can also be used for numbers. Try interchanging between cards and numbers to keep your brain active.

The ALI Method

Exercise: Visualise the *locus* for your image in the quickest time possible.

This exercise tests your ability to think quickly. Have a deck of cards in your hand. As you turn over a playing card, see how quickly you can recall the *locus* for each card. Doing this will help you to think faster and connect visuals more effectively. For a further challenge, instead of spending time thinking of the *locus* image associated with the card, try recalling the associated *locus* immediately instead. The better you get at this, the better you will be at using the ALI method for memorising numbers and cards.

Concentration

Exercise: Find your mental drain point for memorising cards, then memorise for double that time.

How long can you concentrate before your brain starts to fade? Like with the reading concentration exercise, you probably hit a drain point when you try to memorise playing cards. If you get tired after five minutes, then your challenge is to memorise for ten minutes. If you get drained after ten minutes, then try twenty minutes of card memorisation. If you happen to complete a deck of playing cards in that time move on to another deck. If you finish a second deck in that time, go for a third. This exercise is designed to help you build up concentration and remain focused.

Slow Down for Image/Story Creation

Exercise: Instead of memorising quickly, memorise slowly, concentrating on the story you are building using the VAI principle.

This low-down exercise helps you focus on developing the image a lot more clearly and with more depth. The more depth they have, the simpler they will be to recall. I would highly recommend this exercise for those needing to work more on their creativity.

As a general guide, try taking thirty seconds per card when memorising cards. Go slower if you need to.

Story Making

Exercise: Memorise more in one *locus*.

When you're memorising fifty-two cards in fifty-two locations, it takes fifty-two brain processes: that is, you are making up fifty-two stories. Because each story only features one image, it is difficult to make a story that flows: you end up just attaching an image to the *locus* rather than developing a story. By memorising two cards per *locus,* you're now halving the number of stories to remember. Not only that, but the two words can create a small story. If you end up not being able to recall a card, then the second card may prompt you about what the other card was.

There are a few traps with using this technique, though:

- If the VAI principle isn't applied well, the cards may not work as prompts to each other.
- There is a chance that you will mix up the order you're memorising the cards in if the story is not clear enough in its visual and logical order.
- Twenty-six stories is still a lot to remember.

Many championship competitors use three cards per *locus.* This minimises their chances of making mistakes and allows them to remember more.

Advantages of memorising three cards per *locus* include:

- You only need seventeen *loci* to memorise fifty-two cards. This makes it easier to memorise multiple decks of cards.
- You can make a stronger story with three images. This means the story can be more meaningful, which in turn creates engagement for the brain.
- Cards will prompt a forgotten card much more easily, as the story now has a logical order and flow. If a card is missed, then the card either side of it will provide a prompt for recall.

Disadvantages include:

- It takes a slightly longer time to memorise, as there are now three cards in each story.
- If the story isn't made well, then, as in all memorisation, there's a chance of forgetting.

- It may not work for everyone. Some people find it easier to memorise one card per *locus,* as opposed to three.

Exercising your brain to remember four cards per *locus* is, I believe, a great way of improving your memory. It provides that extra challenge of trying to make up a story with four images and tests your creativity, as you are now linking more things together in one location. It is similar to speed reading: by grabbing as many words as you can visualise in one place, then memorising four cards per *locus,* you're involving a greater visual connection with more images.

Advantages are:
- You can develop a strong story with a logical development, making it much harder to forget the sequence of cards once memorised.
- You only need thirteen locations. Having fifty-two locations will now allow you to memorise four decks rather than just one, which is cool!
- You can spend longer memorising the story. This takes away the stress of having to quickly remember fifty-two or twenty-six stories. If you take ten seconds to memorise thirteen stories, that is only 130 seconds (2:10 minutes) to memorise a deck of cards. To memorise in 2:10 minutes using one card per location, you would need to memorise at a speed of 2.5 seconds per card. It is therefore much easier to take a bit longer to make a longer story that makes sense.

The disadvantages are the same as those described for working with three cards per *locus.*

The Peg Words Technique (Major System)
Exercise: Give yourself five minutes to decode as many numbers as you can in the quickest time possible.

The toughest thing to do in memory is to create a memorable image. A good exercise to train your brain to go from step 1 — abstract to step 2 — association is to practise with the Major system of decoding numbers. The best way to do this is to print out a set of numbers and, using the Major system, decode them into images as quickly as you can. Once you've done that, try and make up a story from them. This exercise is great for those who struggle with developing images and are more left-brained in nature. It is the practice of the Yellow Elephant.

Vision Puzzle Exercise

To better understand how the Yellow elephant model works, here's an exercise I developed for one of my leadership classes. It can be conducted with a minimum of six and a maximum of twenty participants, and you will need two one-hundred-piece jigsaw puzzle kits.

Duration: 20 minutes

1. Divide the group into three subgroups. If there are twenty participants, make two groups of eight and a group of four. The two groups of eight are divided as two separate teams. Those in the group of four are the observers. If there are fewer people, just make sure that there are always fewer observers than group participants.
2. Take the observers out of the room, away from the two main groups. Explain to them that their job is to take note of the behaviour of each group as a whole, as well as the behaviour of individuals when trying to piece together the puzzles.
3. Give one group their one-hundred-piece puzzle, along with the final image of what they will be piecing together.
4. Give the other group their one-hundred-piece puzzle, but with no image of what they will be piecing together.

5. The groups now have ten minutes to piece together their puzzles as a team.

6. After ten minutes, gather everyone together for a debrief.

   a. First, ask the group that had the puzzle image how they went working together to construct the puzzle. Did they have any difficulty? What worked? What didn't work? Why?

   b. Now, ask the group with no puzzle image the same questions.

   c. Finally, ask the observers what they observed about the two groups. What were the differences and/or similarities between them? What struggles did they see? What did specific individuals do? And so on.

The aim is to compare how people react when a clear vision is presented and how they react when no clear vision is available. The group discussion should ultimately lead to understanding of the importance of having and effectively communicating vision: most participants will agree that if people don't have a vision of the final piece, it is much more difficult to put the puzzle together. The longer the discussion, the greater capacity you will have to reflect on and compare the two groups.

Occasionally the group without the puzzle image will do better — if they have generated a collective understanding of what the final image is. This could be initiated and driven by a leader within the group. However, the underlying premise remains the same: that is, without a clear vision, it is difficult to work together.

This exercise is a good way of demonstrating the importance for organization of communicating a clear collective vision. Organisations must know how to communicate their vision so that staff members know exactly where and how they fit within the organisation and what the overall aims and goals are. The secret is to use stories and images to inspire and engage staff.

Brain Training for Kids

Kids are amazing. They are like little sponges that soak up information really quickly. Their imaginations are very vivid. Just ask them questions about something they don't know or you think they may not know and observe what they say. Their minds work instinctively in extraordinary ways.

The Linking Game

This is a game I used to play with my daughter years ago to build up her skills in making associations from simple images. It provides practice in the VAI memory principle. For example, I would say a random word such as 'frog' and then another word, 'table', and then get my daughter to make up a story with those two words. The linking game helps develop imagination and creativity and is easy to play anywhere.

Story Making

If you're reading to your child, a great way to build up their creativity is to get them to tell you the story without reading, just by looking at the images. Even though it won't be the same as the written story, you will be amazed at what kids can describe and think of. This can even be done over and over with the same material so the child can learn how to create something new from something they already know.

Mind Mapping

Mind mapping is a great tool for kids to learn and they enjoy the process. One way to use it is to connect their drawings to words. One of my clients had brought in their six-year-old son who was on medication for ADHD and had been told his memory wasn't very good after being assessed at school. After a few weeks showing him and his parents how mind mapping can be used to connect both sides of the brain, his whole learning pattern changed and he gradually got better and better at school.

Speed Reading

Teach your child to read with their finger. It is an essential skill and will help them to focus and prepare for real speed reading techniques when they are older. It will assist them to form images when they are older so they can quickly progress to reading in large chunks. If they can read, then the next step is to teach them to chunk two words at a time and to try and visualise them rather than read them. If they practise this, they will be speed reading with enhanced comprehension at a very young age.

Memory Fuel

Physical and mental training is not the only way to enhance memory. What you put in your body can play a huge part as well. A healthy body is a healthy mind, and a healthy mind is a healthy body. When thinking about nutrition, we should think both in terms of physical health and in terms of brain and mental health. More and more research is revealing the positive effects of omega-3 fatty acids, and particularly docosahexaenoic acid, or DHA, on memory. Blackseed oil is another natural wonder, not only for memory improvement, but also for curing many illnesses and overall wellbeing. Educating yourself on the latest research into nutrition and brain health will pay off!

The MIDAS Study

One of the most interesting studies on DHA to be published recently is the Memory Improvement with Docosahexaenoic Acid Study (MIDAS). The large, randomised and placebo-controlled study found that healthy people with memory complaints who took 900 mg of DSM algal DHA capsules for six months had almost double the reduction in errors on a test that measures learning and memory performance versus those who took a placebo, a benefit roughly equivalent to having the learning and memory skills of someone three years younger. The results of the MIDAS study represent an important breakthrough in the area of brain health.

Yet, despite the importance of DHA, most people eating a Western diet consume low amounts of it. 'The average Australian consumes less than half the recommended dietary intake of long-chain omega-3 fatty acids,' remarks dietician Melanie McGrice. 'With up to one third of baby boomers in Australia likely to experience a gradual decline in cognitive function as they age, MIDAS is significant, because it shows for the first time that taking 900 mg of algal DHA daily may have a very meaningful and important impact on cognitive function in the ageing population.'

'We have known for a long time based on the strong body of epidemiological research that DHA may play an important role in cognitive function, particularly in the ageing population,' says Dr Karin Yurko-Mauro, project lead of MIDAS. 'With MIDAS, we now have clinical evidence to indicate that 900 mg of algal DHA improves memory and learning in ageing adults.'

Most commonly found in fish, more and more foods are now being fortified with omega-3 DHA. Although fish are a nutritious source of omega-3 DHA and other nutrients, people are not consuming enough fish to get significant amounts of DHA in their diet.

The source of DHA used in MIDAS was a vegetarian and sustainable algal DHA produced by DSM, and marketed to consumers under the brand name of life'sDHA™. Foods, beverages, and supplements fortified with life'sDHA™ are available in supermarkets.

Key Points

- Focus on story development by using the VAI memory principle. Brain training without this won't help as it is the image and story creation component that is the key for memory improvement.
- Be persistent. You may feel like nothing is happening or you're just not benefiting from training your brain using the above exercises. Physical change also occurs in due time, so think the same and don't expect instant results.
- Good nutrition can also assist your mental health. Look at things like DHA Omega-3 or even Blackseed Oil which is a natural wonder for not just memory improvement, but curing many illnesses and improving overall wellbeing.

Testing Your Memory

'Memorising in youth is like engraving on stone and memorising when old is like engraving on water.'

— PROPHET MUHAMMED

NOW THAT YOU'VE LEARNT the techniques and understood how they can be applied, it's time to test your learning. See how you go with the reading and memory tests that follow. You can revisit them over time to see how you improve. There are also additional challenges added for those who want to take that extra step and memorise more.

Finally, remember before you start to memorise anything to think about how you intend to approach memorisation, and remember that you can either do it the hard way or the fun way! It is up to you to practise, learn from mistakes and explore how memory techniques can be applied in different situations. Enjoy!

Reading Test

Read the following passage as quickly as you can, using your speed reading techniques, and then answer the comprehension questions that follow. Time yourself as well, so you can monitor how your reading speed is improving.

Is Leadership Failing?

CRAIG DENT

This question is being asked more often these days. Those from whom we expect leadership are seemingly failing, and this is not constrained to any one particular sector — many examples in the daily news serve as a frequent reminder that, increasingly, leadership is failing.

For too many organisations, developing and sustaining the capability of leadership remains elusive, an unresolved strategic issue. This is despite the reality that we have more leadership development opportunities today than ever before, delivered through a variety of methods, supported by more than four hundred and fifty-six million searchable items on Google and more than ninety-eight thousand leadership resources available online through Amazon, for example. So what's not working?

The answer is as complex as successful and sustained leadership is itself.

Mainstream leadership programs, which take a traditional approach with theory, debate, discussion and action-based projects, certainly have their place. Indeed, this is where the journey of building leadership capabilities starts. These programs build knowledge in a safe yet challenging environment for participants. However, this approach can best be described as one-off training.

Organisations are often quick to send their management to leadership programs as if it will magically address the organisation's issues. The reality is that while the organisation will initially see improved performances as a dividend for their investment in the training, it is also true that this improvement will generally not be sustained.

The unfortunate truth is that the core issues will re-emerge, unless the organisation's leadership is part of an authentic leadership development program of constant exposure to knowledge, different views, development opportunities, self-reflection and — frankly — hard work by the individuals themselves, over a prolonged period of time.

Through leadership training, individuals can build and fill their leadership toolbox with the core competencies of leadership. Once they have had the opportunity to practise and refine the use of those tools, a very small number of individuals will go through a significant and permanent change. For them, the changes — in their thinking, focus, reflection and action — will be widespread. It is this time that sees true leadership capability emerge; this is where you see and hear a tangible difference — and the difference is the beginning of the authentic leadership journey.

What is often not understood about leadership is that it is developed, not trained per se; it requires a long-term development plan and supporting program. Leadership training has a vital place as the first stage, but the journey does not end there.

Research is revealing more and more about the value of individual journeys of discovery for leaders. This process involves unpicking one's past and examining life events, with a focus on how those events affected and how individuals see and reflect on events that play out in organisations daily. Importantly, leadership development uncovers how and why individuals react the way they do. Once the 'lens' through which they see, hear and react to event is understood, authentic leadership is possible.

Exploring one's ancestry, discovering stories of hardship and triumph, is yet to be commonly embraced as part of a deeper leadership journey of development. However, ancestral discoveries generally have a profound impact on

an individual who is working to understand themselves —
this can only lead to greater authenticity.

Furthermore, in the shift from conventional to post-conventional thinking, a leader will find true comfort in
reve   ng themselves to those who choose to follow them,
and more broadly to those who may also have leadership
aspirations. Revealing one's true self in our stories, our
flaws, our learning, our failures and our successes, for all
to see, discuss, reflect on and perhaps debate, is immensely
challenging. This is part of the reason why so few ever reach
this point of authentic leadership.

Given the repeated failings of leadership today, there is
no better time than now for leaders or those with aspirations
to leadership, irrespective of the context or sector, to be
willing to try a new frontier, the frontier of self-reflection.

The other important aspect of this post-conventional
thinking is for a leader to listen to others' perspectives about
their leadership style, methods, and engagement. When was
the last time you received or even sought feedback about
your performance as a leader from those you work for, work
with or lead?

The reality is that few do. Jay M Jackman and Myra H
Strober, in their article 'Fear of Feedback' published in the
Harvard Business Review in April 2003 state that:

> this fear of feedback doesn't come into play just during
> annual reviews. At least half the executives with whom
> we've worked never ask for feedback. Many expect the
> worst: heated arguments, impossible demands, or even
> threats of dismissal. So rather than seek feedback, people
> avoid the truth and instead continue to try to guess what
> their bosses think.

Fears and assumptions about feedback often manifest
themselves in psychologically maladaptive behaviours

such as procrastination, denial, brooding, jealousy, and self-sabotage. But there's hope. Those who learn to adapt to feedback can free themselves from old patterns. They can learn to acknowledge negative emotions, constructively reframe fear and criticism, develop realistic goals, create support systems, and reward themselves for achievements along the way.

When was the last time you took advantage of a diagnostic tool to better understand who you are?

The diagnostic tools in isolation are insightful; however, using more than one, and ideally three, provides for compelling insights into your leadership capabilities and allows you to identify what to focus on to further improve your leadership capabilities. It is for these reasons that I recommend completing more than one.

The diagnostic tools I recommend are:

— Myers-Briggs Type Indicator (MBTI)

— Human Synergistics

— Leadership Development Profile

Myers-Briggs Type Indicator (MBTI)

The MBTI is attributed to mother and daughter Katherine Cook Briggs and Isabel Briggs Myers respectively and correctly. However, they had drawn on the work of Carl Jung, who originally published his work *Psychological Types* in 1921.

The mother and daughter team were successful in the establishment of an assessment questionnaire, which was first published in 1962 and has become one of the world's most used diagnostic tools.

The MTBI measures an individual's psychological preferences; in other words, it measures how you perceive events and make decisions.

Human Synergistics

Created by Dr J Clayton Lafferty and Dr Robert A Cooke forty years ago, the Human Synergistics Circumplex provides individuals and organisations with an assessment of responses to questions broken into twelve styles and grouped into (1) Constructive, (2) Passive/Defensive or (3) Aggressive/Defensive overall styles. This is presented in a circular format, hence the 'circumplex'.

The outcome of the diagnostic tool enables both individuals and organisations to see the perceptions of others over a period of time, measure the change efforts and better understand the respective styles of the organisation's employees in a powerful and engaging way.

Leadership Development Profile

The Leadership Development Framework is based on the Heifetz adaptive leadership model and on the work of Rooke and Torbert on action enquiry and is underpinned by the research discussed in their article 'Seven Transformations of Leadership', published in the *Harvard Business Review* 2006.

Rooke and Torbert say in their 'Seven Transformations of Leadership' article that 'great leaders are differentiated not by their personality or philosophy but by their action logic — how they interpret their own and others' behaviour and how they maintain power or protect against threats.'

While all three tools provide insight into the individual's leadership styles and methods, the three combined form a powerful tool for those who take their development and leadership seriously. The tools provide more value if conducted over consecutive years for comparison and measurement purposes.

Who do you think of when asked to name a leader who inspires you? Think of someone in your community or sector, not the leadership celebrities who get quoted continuously:

someone you know, someone who is local to your community. Chances are that you struggled to name someone. Is this not in itself an indication that things must change?

Evidence is increasingly emerging that people's leadership success can be accelerated and sustained at greater levels, provided that the leadership development pathway is customised. This reflects the fact that leadership development is about adapting learning to a person's particular needs based on specific category assessments. Yet what is being done to harness this within our organisations today? More specifically, what are you doing to harness this reality today?

Concerned about how this may stack up as a business case? By identifying the obstacles to leadership development that are restricting career pathways and limiting organisational performance, organisations will be able to identify and develop their leaders in a more customised and efficient manner, avoiding the costly errors in recruitment and selection processes along with the ongoing organisational challenge of retaining the right leadership talent.

Assessing a person's leadership capabilities and needs early enables organisational success and competitive advantage. Benefits will be widespread and material.

The more challenging and frankly concerning question is: what if we don't embrace a new method that results in the right leadership talent being identified, retained and placed in the most beneficial roles within the organisation, and our competitors do? The reality is that your organisation will fail, just as we see so many leaders failing today.

Are you prepared to confront yourself in a way that makes you truly vulnerable in order to enable your leadership capabilities to evolve into that increasingly rare state of authenticity? Will you be courageous enough to lead?

1574 words

Comprehension Test

1. Organisations increasingly self-identifying that the identification, retention and development of leadership capabilities remains an ...
   a. undisputed strategic issue
   b. undeniable truth
   c. unresolved strategic issue
   d. untapped resource

2. How many searchable items are there about leadership on Google?
   a. 98 thousand
   b. 456 million
   c. 57 thousand
   d. 1.4 million

3. An increase in performance will be generally sustained through leadership training. True or false?

4. Ancestral discoveries can lead to:
   a. greater authenticity
   b. knowing your future
   c. your disaster
   d. discovering your past

5. The article 'Fear of Feedback' was written by:
   a. Peter D Foreman and Shelly K Donald
   b. D Mustaine and M Friedman
   c. Jay M Jackman and Myra H Strober
   d. Shane K Roger

6. MBTI stands for ...
   a. Mark Beaver Type Index
   b. Myers-Briggs Type Index

c. Myers-Briggs Type Indicator

d. Myers-Briggs Test Index

7. The Human Synergistic Circumplex provides individuals and organisations with an assessment of responses to questions broken into …

a. nine styles

b. thirteen styles

c. Twenty-seven styles

d. Twelve styles

8. The Leadership Development Framework is based on which leadership model?

a. The Rupert model of sustainability

b. Heifetz adaptive leadership model

c. Clawson's Diamond model of leadership

d. Blake and Mouton's leadership grid

9. Assessing a person's leadership capabilities and needs early:

a. allows the organisation to recruit accordingly

b. becomes an enabler for organisational success and competitive advantage

c. provides a benchmark for all other leaders

d. lowers the chances of organisational sustainability

10. The unfortunate truth is that the core issues will re-emerge, unless the organisation's leadership is a part of _____ leadership development.

a. a robust

b. sustainable

c. authentic

d. ongoing

Solutions: 1. c; 2. b; 3. False; 4. a; 5. c; 6. c; 7. d; 8. b; 9. b; 10. c

Memory Tests
Numbers Memory Test

Memorise the following numbers. Get a friend to test you.

4 3 9 2 3 1 7 8 2 9 3 9 5 7 7 8 8 5 4 9 7 9 9 7 6 9 8 6 2 3 7 0 2 3 5
6 0 3 2 0 2 9 5 4 6 9 8 3 8 8 6 8 2 8 3 8 3 1 3 0 4 3 2 6 9 7 4 3 9 3
5 3 8 7 0 2 1 5 6 6 2 0 1 6 7 4 1 9 8 1 8 5 2 9 9 5 2 1 7 2 5 7 8 4 5
3 1 0 9 3 3 9 3 6 2 9 2 0 7 4 6 7 8 8 5 3 3 4 9 8 3 2 3 0 1 5 4 5 4 4
0 6 2 2 1 5 8 1 9 4 7 8 4 9 4 4 5 0 8 9 5 1 0 1 3 3 5 1 8 8 2 0 8 1 8
3 2 1 8 5 1 1 8 8 5 1 5 4 6 6 7 7 2 7 8 0 6 1 9 2 2 0 4 2 5 2 2 5 5 0
3 1 7 6 0 4 2 6 9 9 4 7 2 8 3 8 6 9 7 4 2 0 0 6 9 7 8 8 7 1 4 5 7 6 9
1 5 8 9 8 4 7 2 2 9 8 6 7 5 9 3 3 2 0 0 3 5 6 7 3 4 6 6 3 7 5 9 8 1 0

Words Memory Test

Memorise the following words.

marble	trampoline	lard	blouse	knife
eye	samurai	seamstress	toy	talkback
font	ladybird	eraser	roundabout	eulogy
shadow	mineral	parliament	whirlwind	family
language	bolero	index	yoyo	elevator
orchestra	lace	employer	noodle	glue
mermaid	ensemble	telex	carbon	period
driftwood	equator	outback	choir	uncle
onion	deacon	engine	flame	quorum
wildlife	quota	haze	allergy	nexus

To-do List Memory Test

Memorise the following to-do list.

1. Take the rubbish out
2. Buy the groceries
3. Buy the newspaper
4. Pay bills

5. Go for a walk
6. Sing a song
7. Prepare presentation
8. Go to the gym
9. Get car washed
10. Buy birthday present for Craig

Additional Challenges
Dates Memory Test

Memorise the following dates and fictional events.

1985	Flash Gordon trips over himself
2050	First dog on the Moon
1631	Three women have triplets
1367	Man overcomes knee injury
1220	Doctor says time travel possible
1738	Elephant makes fart sound
1886	Dumbo's ears get stretched
1454	Alien lands on Venus
1718	Singer forgets own name
1574	Conquest of Gilligan's Island
1511	Comedian tells a funny joke
2022	Richard Branson trapped in space
1190	Kids visit a zoo
1087	Earthquake of Babylon
1377	Hotcakes start to sell — like hotcakes
1479	Tennis racquet made
1206	Coffee makes people fall asleep
1516	Horses go on a rampage
1059	Sword developed for spreading butter
1538	Loyalty card found on street
1934	Cat falls out of a tree
1655	Child sees dead people
1675	Heavy metal music invented

2082   Man uses a pen to write
1182   Rubbish taken out
2042   Internet reaches 100 mbps in Melbourne
1846   Play is written about Shakespeare
1357   Woman busted picking her nose in public
1211   Politician tells the truth
1027   Secret herbs and spices invented

Poetry Memory Test

Memorise the following poem.

Hearken to the reed-flute, how it complains,
    Lamenting its banishment from its home:
'Ever since they tore me from my osier bed,
    My plaintive notes have moved men and women to tears.

I burst my breast, striving to give vent to sighs,
    And to express the pangs of my yearning for my home.
He who abides far away from his home
    Is ever longing for the day he shall return.

My wailing is heard in every throng,
    In concert with them that rejoice and them that weep.
Each interprets my notes in harmony with his own feelings,
    But not one fathoms the secrets of my heart.

My secrets are not alien from my plaintive notes,
    Yet they are not manifest to the sensual eye and ear.
Body is not veiled from soul, neither soul from body,
    Yet no man hath ever seen a soul.'

This plaint of the flute is fire, not mere air.
    Let him who lacks this fire be accounted dead!
'Tis the fire of love that inspires the flute,
    'Tis the ferment of love that possesses the wine.

The flute is the confidant of all unhappy lovers;
  Yea, its strains lay bare my inmost secrets.
Who hath seen a poison and an antidote like the flute?
  Who hath seen a sympathetic consoler like the flute?

The flute tells the tale of love's bloodstained path,
  It recounts the story of Majnun's love toils.
None is privy to these feelings save one distracted,
  As ear inclines to the whispers of the tongue.

Through grief my days are as labour and sorrow,
  My days move on, hand in hand with anguish.
Yet, though my days vanish thus, 'tis no matter,
  Do thou abide, O Incomparable Pure One!

But all who are not fishes are soon tired of water;
  And they who lack daily bread find the day very long;
So the 'Raw' comprehend not the state of the 'Ripe;'
  Therefore it behoves me to shorten my discourse.

Arise, O son! Burst thy bonds and be free!
  How long wilt thou be captive to silver and gold?
Though thou pour the ocean into thy pitcher,
  It can hold no more than one day's store.

The pitcher of the desire of the covetous never fills,
  The oyster-shell fills not with pearls till it is content;
Only he whose garment is rent by the violence of love
  Is wholly pure from covetousness and sin.

Hail to thee, then, O LOVE, sweet madness!
  Thou who healest all our infirmities!
Who art the physician of our pride and self-conceit!
  Who art our Plato and our Galen!

Love exalts our earthly bodies to heaven,
    And makes the very hills to dance with joy!
O lover, 'twas love that gave life to Mount Sinai,
    When 'it quaked, and Moses fell down in a swoon.'

Did my Beloved only touch me with his lips,
    I too, like the flute, would burst out in melody.
But he who is parted from them that speak his tongue,
    Though he possess a hundred voices, is perforce dumb.

When the rose has faded and the garden is withered,
    The song of the nightingale is no longer to be heard.
The BELOVED is all in all, the lover only veils Him;
    The BELOVED is all that lives, the lover a dead thing.

When the lover feels no longer LOVE's quickening,
    He becomes like a bird who has lost its wings. Alas!
How can I retain my senses about me,
    When the BELOVED shows not the light of His countenance?

LOVE desires that this secret should be revealed,
    For if a mirror reflects not, of what use is it?
Knowest thou why thy mirror reflects not?
    Because the rust has not been scoured from its face.

If it were purified from all rust and defilement,
    It would reflect the shining of the SUN Of GOD.
O friends, ye have now heard this tale,
    Which sets forth the very essence of my case.
              — Mewalan Jalaluddin Rumi

Human Body Memory Test

Memorise the bones of the human body

Carnial bones (8):
- frontal bone
- parietal bone (2)
- temporal bone (2)

Facial bones (14):
- mandible
- maxilla (2)
- nasal bone (2)
- lacrimal bone (2)

In the middle ears (6):
- malleus (2)
- incus (2)
- stapes (2)

In the vertebral column (24):
- cervical vertebrae (7)
- thoracic vertebrae (12)
- lumbar vertebrae (5)

In the forearms (4):
- radium (2)
- ulna (2)

In the hands, excluding sesamoid bones (54):
- carpal (wrist) bones (16):
  — scaphoid bone (2)
  — lunate bone (2)
  — triquetrum bone (2)
  — pisiform bone (2)
  — trapezium (2)
  — trapezoid bone (2)

- metacarpus (palm) bones (10):
  - metacarpal bones (5 × 2)
- digits of the hands (finger bones or phalanges) (28):
  - proximal phalanges (5 × 2)
  - intermediate phalanges (4 × 2)
  - distal phalanges (5 × 2)

In the legs (6):
- patella (2)
- tibia (2)
- fibula (2)

In the feet, excluding sesamoid bones (52):
- tarsal (ankle) bones (14):
  - talus (2)
  - navicular bone (2)
  - medial cuneiform bone (2)
  - intermediate cuneiform bone (2)
  - lateral cuneiform bone (2)
- metatarsus bones (10):
  - metatarsal bone (5 × 2)
- digits of the feet (toe bones or phalanges) (28):
  - proximal phalanges (5 × 2)
  - intermediate phalanges (4 × 2)

Key Points
- Always keep challenging yourself. The test in this chapter should be a good challenge to improve your use of memory techniques.
- Seek out other material to memorise and have a good crack at it. You'll be surprised what you'll find yourself able to do!
- Enjoy memorising. It should not be stressful. If it is, then ask yourself how you can make it more fun instead.

Acknowledgements

I would like to first thank God (Allah) Almighty for making all of this happen and for giving me the gift of life. Thanks to my mother, my father and my grandparents, who have been my greatest inspiration and influences. I thank my dear friends who supported me along my journey and who also gave me their valuable time to make this book even more memorable. In particular, Metin Hassan, one of the most creative people I've ever met. I never would have thought your little interest in memory would have led me here! Thanks, buddy.

I thank the people I've worked with and gained great insight into memory: Jennifer Goddard and Bill Jarrard for their tireless work in this field (you guys are an inspiration!); Tony Buzan for introducing me to the world of personal development, memory and mind mapping (you've really helped me understand what memory is really all about. I can't live without Mind Mapping now!); Dominic O'Brien for being my memory sports inspiration; my fellow memory colleague Chris Lyons, from whom I learnt a lot about professionalism, delivering engaging workshops and enjoying working in this field; Dr Janusz Tanas for mentoring me and guiding me in the right direction in my business; Mark Dobson for his friendship and support and for making me a better speaker; Gavin Blake from Fever Picture for his creativity and illustrations (you're an absolute gun!); DSM and Swisse Vitamins for their support and also for providing research into memory products; Francesca and the crew at Crohn's and Colitis Australia for their faith in me as a Celebrity Ambassador.

I'd also like to thank the National and World Memory Championship competitors, who are a great bunch of people. I'm happy to be part of such an awesome global community.

Thank you to the publishers for believing in my ability to write this book and for supporting me through tough times. You guys are truly amazing!

And finally to my wife, Monique, and our three kids: thanks for putting up with me. Love you all.